AMERICAN WAR LIBRARY

★ ★ ★ ★

★ The Vietnam War ★

LIFE AS A POW

by Diana Saenger
and Bradley Steffens

Lucent Books, P.O. Box 289011, San Diego, CA 92198-9011

Titles in The American War Library series include:

World War II
Hitler and the Nazis
Kamikazes
Leaders and Generals
Life as a POW
Life of an American Soldier in
  Europe
Strategic Battles in Europe
Strategic Battles in the Pacific
The War at Home
Weapons of War

The Civil War
Leaders of the North and South
Life Among the Soldiers and
  Cavalry
Lincoln and the Abolition of
  Slavery

Strategic Battles
Weapons of War

The Persian Gulf War
Leaders and Generals
Life of an American Soldier
The War Against Iraq
Weapons of War

The Vietnam War
A History of U.S. Involvement
The Home Front: Americans
  Protest the War
Leaders and Generals
Life as a POW
Life of an American Soldier
Weapons of War

Cover photo: U.S. Air Force pilot Lt. Hayden Lockhardt is captured by a North Vietnamese militiaman after he was forced to eject from his disabled jet over Hanoi.

Library of Congress Cataloging-in-Publication Data

Saenger, Diana, 1946–   , and Steffens, Bradley, 1955–
    Life as a POW / By Diana Saenger and Bradley Steffens.
        p. cm.—(American war library. Vietnam War)
    ISBN 1-56006-716-0
    1. Vietnamese Conflict, 1961–1975—Prison and prisons, North
  Vietnamese—Juvenile literature. 2. Prisoners of war—United States
  —Juvenile literature. [1. Vietnamese Conflict, 1961–1975—Prisoners
  of war—History—20th century.] I. Title. II. Series.
  DS559.5 .S235 2001
  959.704'37—dc21
                                                                    00-011983

Printed in the U.S.A.

★ Contents ★

A Nation Forged by War

The United States, like many nations, was forged and defined by war. Despite Benjamin Franklin's opinion that "There never was a good war or a bad peace," the United States owes its very existence to the War of Independence, one to which Franklin wholeheartedly subscribed. The country forged by war in 1776 was tempered and made stronger by the Civil War in the 1860s.

The Texas Revolution, the Mexican-American War, and the Spanish-American War expanded the country's borders and gave it overseas possessions. These wars made the United States a world power, but this status came with a price, as the nation became a key but reluctant player in both World War I and World War II.

Each successive war further defined the country's role on the world stage. Following World War II, U.S. foreign policy redefined itself to focus on the role of defender, not only of the freedom of its own citizens, but also of the freedom of people everywhere. During the cold war that followed World War II until the collapse of the Soviet Union, defending the world meant fighting communism. This goal, manifested in the Korean and Vietnam conflicts, proved elusive, and soured the American public on its achievability. As the United States emerged as the world's sole superpower, American foreign policy has been guided less by national interest and more on protecting international human rights. But as involvement in Somalia and Kosovo prove, this goal has been equally elusive.

As a result, the country's view of itself changed. Bolstered by victories in World Wars I and II, Americans first relished the role of protector. But, as war followed war in a seemingly endless procession, Americans began to doubt their leaders, their motives, and themselves. The Vietnam War especially caused people to question the validity of sending its young people to die in places where they were not particularly wanted and for people who did not seem especially grateful.

While the most obvious changes brought about by America's wars have been geopolitical in nature, many other aspects of society have been touched. War often does not bring about change directly, but acts instead like the catalyst in a chemical reaction, accelerating changes already in progress.

Some of these changes have been societal. The role of women in the United States had been slowly changing, but World War II put thousands into the workforce and into uniform. They might have gone back to being housewives after the war, but equality, once experienced, would not be forgotten.

Likewise, wars have accelerated technological change. The necessity for faster airplanes and a more destructive bomb led to the development of jet planes and nuclear energy. Artificial fibers developed for parachutes in the 1940s were used in the clothing of the 1950s.

Lucent Books' American War Library covers key wars in the development of the nation. Each war is covered in several volumes, to allow for more detail, context, and to provide volumes on often neglected subjects, such as the kamikazes of World War II, or weapons used in the Civil War. As with all Lucent Books, notes, annotated bibliographies, and appendixes such as glossaries give students a launching point for further research. In addition, sidebars and archival photographs enhance the text. Together, each volume in The American War Library will aid students in understanding how America's wars have shaped and changed its politics, economics, and society.

The Longest War in American History

From 1961 to 1973 the United States committed more than half a million troops to the Vietnam War in Southeast Asia. An astonishing fifty-eight thousand American soldiers and civilians died in the twelve-year conflict. More than eight hundred U.S. military and civilian men and women became prisoners of war (POWs) after capture by the North Vietnamese army or the Viet Cong (VC). These POWs spent as many as eight years in the camps enduring inadequate food, physical torture, and isolation. More than one hundred U.S. POWs died in captivity.

Soldiers were not the only Americans imprisoned. Civilians and foreign nationals such as medical personnel, civilian contractors, and missionaries who assisted the U.S. forces also were taken prisoner by the North Vietnamese forces. One hundred twenty-one civilians, including female missionaries and nurses, were killed or imprisoned.

The Horrors of War Came Quickly

The United States became involved in the conflict in Vietnam because North Vietnam wanted a Chinese Communist controlled government and South Vietnam wanted independence from Communist rule. In 1955 the United States, which supported the South's efforts to remain anti-Communist, sent military personnel to train the South Vietnamese to defend themselves against the North Vietnamese armies. When the first two American advisors, Major Dale Buis and Sergeant Chester Ovnand, died on July 8, 1959, during a VC raid on an American mess hall, President Eisenhower and his administration reassessed American involvement in the Vietnam conflict. In 1961, outgoing President Eisenhower privately told his successor, John Kennedy, that the new president probably would have to commit American ground troops to Southeast Asia. Once in office, Kennedy reached the same conclusion. He ordered more American troops to Vietnam in an

The Differences and Realities of This War

The Vietnam War was the third conflict to which American forces had been sent in just twenty years. In the 1940s, the United States had fought in Europe and the Pacific against the Axis powers in World War II. In the 1950s, American ground troops joined the South Koreans to fend off attacks from North Korea. Vietnam presented a challenge to the American military that it had never faced before. American soldiers had not been trained to fight the kind of guerrilla-style war that the North Vietnamese preferred. In guerrilla warfare, the enemy strikes from concealed positions rather than from a concentrated battlefront. By using guerrilla tactics, the North Vietnamese army was able to avoid a direct confrontation with the American military's greatest asset—its superior weaponry and firepower. In addition, the North Vietnamese knew the terrain better than Americans did. This gave the guerrilla warriors an important advantage over the American troops.

Because Congress never declared war against North Vietnam, government officials failed to convince many average Americans of the war's importance. Knowing that many members of Congress and a large segment of the population were skeptical about increasing the war effort, the American presidents who presided over the war tried to keep some aspects of it secret.

The decision not to declare war also influenced the conduct of the North Vietnamese government toward American

President Eisenhower (top) informed President-elect John F. Kennedy that he probably would have to commit ground troops to Vietnam.

effort to hold off the Communist invasion of the South. Although the United States became more involved, it still never declared war against North Vietnam.

POWs. The North Vietnamese maintained that the provisions set forth in the 1949 Geneva Convention Diplomatic Conference in Switzerland regarding the treatment of prisoners of war did not apply to Americans in Vietnam because the United States had never formally declared war. Insisting that captured Americans were "war criminals," not prisoners of war, the North Vietnamese treated POWs brutally. In his book *Captive Warriors,* U.S. Air Force Major Samuel Johnson remembers being tortured immediately after arriving in camp. He writes:

I opened my eyes to see thin shafts of light that seeped in through cracked window shutters and then bled quickly into the gray dimness. The torture room was empty now, except for my mangled form lying in a corner like a tossed-out carcass. The concrete floor was mottled with splotches of dried blood mixed with layers of grime. Peeling paint hung from stark white walls like limp streamers left over from a party in a shop of horrors.[1]

One Geneva Convention rule mandated that a list of captured men and women be published. No list was ever released. It took some families many years to learn that their missing soldier was alive and in prison. In the beginning and at other times during the war the VC refused to allow the International Committee of the Red Cross to inspect camps.

If they had inspected the camps, the Red Cross would have discovered very quickly, just as the incoming prisoners did, that torture rooms were ready and waiting. "At the Heartbreak Hotel section, the welcoming committee let you know they had other plans for you," said Captain Ron Bliss. "You could look at this place and hear the screams of fifty years because it was a hard place."[2]

One POW who had been a prisoner in Germany during World War II told Commander Stockdale there was no comparison to the Vietnamese prison. Stockdale said, "He told me, 'There I was hungry and cold so there was only wear and tear on my body. They didn't want anything. They didn't want any propaganda or military secrets, they knew all that. They left us alone. Here, it's wear and tear on the nervous system, and that's entirely different.'"[3]

POWs returned home suffering from bouts of depression, listlessness, or inattention. Friends, new employers, and family often could not understand why the GIs could not forget about their past and rejoice that they were home. These people could never understand. None of them had lived as a POW.

Chapter 1

Face to Face with the Enemy

By April 1969 American and South Vietnamese pilots were making thirty-six hundred flying missions a day against North Vietnamese targets. Although the United States had modern planes and skilled pilots, the planes were vulnerable to missile attack, which made American pilots particularly prone to becoming POWs. Even the highly advanced and extremely fast (Mach 2) F-4 Phantom used by the air force, marine, and navy air wings could not escape danger from North Vietnamese missiles obtained from the Soviet Union.

Once a plane was hit, most of the pilots stayed with the plane as long as they could before pushing the ejection button. Pilots often suffered injuries when they were thrust up and out of the cockpit. For example, on August 26, 1967, U.S. Air Force Major George Everett Day ejected from his plane, breaking his arm in three places, dislocating his knee, and causing a blood clot in his eye that temporarily blinded him. He hit the ground unconscious.

Nowhere to Run

Because the North Vietnamese could see the pilot's parachute as it floated down from the sky, they usually captured the ejected pilots quickly. Some pilots managed to stay hidden for a few hours or days, but the dense forests of North Vietnam made it difficult for the pilots to determine where they were. They knew, however, that they were in enemy territory. Every place the pilots ejected—rice paddies, villages, and jungles—was an active battlefield. Many areas were booby-trapped with *punji* stakes dipped in poison and placed in carefully hidden pits. "Bouncing Betty" land mines, designed to blow up on contact, hung in the brush at crotch level.

The jungle contained natural hazards as well. Snakes, red ants, scorpions, and leeches abounded. Malaria-bearing mosquitoes buzzed in the air. Even the soil

Even the advanced F-4 Phantom could not escape the danger posed by North Vietnamese missiles.

presented dangers. Many soldiers suffered from jungle rot, a condition created when cuts or scratches became infected by microbes living in the wet ground. The downed pilots knew the dangers that surrounded them, and some were so badly injured from the ejection that they were unsure whether they would be better off dead or alive. Major Douglas Peterson carefully weighed his options before deciding to survive. "I was rather severely injured," he later wrote. "I had a broken arm, broken shoulder and broken leg. My first decision was whether or not I wanted to live or die. It was a conscious process. I had my .38 [pistol] there and had it out, but I opted not to pull the trigger, and it would have been an easy thing to do."4

Reality of War

Once soldiers were captured—sometimes dazed, confused, or semiconscious—they saw for the first time the faces of the Vietnamese soldiers or peasants who found them. In his book *Beyond Survival*, U.S. Navy Captain Gerald Coffee explained his first reaction when he was found. He wrote:

> For the first time now, I confronted my enemy face to face, an enemy that until now had been an abstract collage of Viet Cong, headlines of war, the Ho Chi Minh Trail, green jungle tops, road junctions on maps, and toy sampans on counterpane mirrors below. Now he had come alive and was real. These were men and boys of flesh and blood making hostile animal noises and gestures to me.

> I was more confused than ever. War was supposed to be clean—mechanical and technical, soldier versus soldier, rocket against tank, missile against plane, all crisp and decisive. Instead, I felt like some helpless cornered prey about to be pounced upon by a pack of savage animals as soon as they had sniffed out my fear.5

A Friendly Gesture among the Savagery

Occasionally friendly villagers were allowed to approach the prisoners. As Captain Gerald Coffee was marched to prison through a small village, he recalled such an incident. Two women carrying *chogi* sticks or shoulder poles, approached the guards and apparently voiced their displeasure at how the prisoner was being treated. The women offered Coffee some tea, inquired through sign language to find out he had three children and another on the way, then moved on to leave his fate in the hands of less friendly forces. He writes in his book *Beyond Survival*:

> They moved closer cautiously for a better look at the "black-hearted American air pirate," as I was to be called frequently in the future. . . . Their little black eyes sparkled in the light, belying the tiredness of the sagging skin around them. They held no youthful fervor and certainly no hatred. The gentleness of one of the women's touch as she reached up to test the tightness of the rope around my neck transcended the political and ideological conflicts that led us both to this unlikely nocturnal encounter.

Questions raced through the captured soldiers' minds. They wondered whether they would be spared or killed. Would their captors show compassion or cruelty? Would they ever see their loved ones again? Coffee recalled some of the thoughts that flashed through his mind: "Would civility overcome the darkest animal instincts in us all, the hatred that I could see clearly in their eyes? But it was not hatred alone. Their eyes also reflected the same excited curiosity, and even some of the fear that I knew must be clearly evident in my own. Would I look into those eyes and kill if I had the upper hand?"[6]

Americans had no choice but to find out. They could only guess what kinds of torture lay ahead for them.

Hated, Scorned, and Beaten

When captured, pilots were relieved of their flight suits, boots, and other gear. Their watches and wedding rings were removed. Even the "combat wallet" containing a military ID card and a Geneva Convention card (to distinguish a fighting man from a spy) was taken. Some pilots carried "blood chits," cards written in several Southeast Asian languages that offered a reward for the safe return of the pilot to American forces.

Stripped of their uniforms, most POWs were dressed in traditional Vietnamese garments that resembled black pajamas. Some pilots were left in their underwear or trousers, but few had shoes. The lucky ones were given rubber sandals made from old tire treads.

Many POWs were blindfolded as they were led to their prison camps. Often the North Vietnamese staged mock execu-

tions along the way. After capture, Lieutenant Commander Hugh Al Stafford was blindfolded, led to a trench, and forced to kneel. He heard the sound of metal on

Almost immediately after being captured, pilots were relieved of their flight suit and all other gear and personal effects.

metal as the Vietnamese militiamen loaded their weapons. He waited silently to be killed and finally heard the click of a camera shutter. When he flinched, his captors laughed. When his blindfold was removed, he saw the laughing faces of the mock firing squad.

Major Samuel Johnson also thought he had only moments to live during his mock execution. He said in the film *Return with Honor:* "They took us out to a firing squad of five guys. They pointed their rifles at me, pulled the clips and the leader said 'fire.' When the click, click, click sounded and I was still alive, I laughed, but for the first time I realized how hard I had been praying that the Lord was on my side."[7]

Most prisoners went to the Hoa Lo Penitentiary in Hanoi, which was centrally located in the populated region of North Vietnam. A few prison camps were within a twenty-mile radius of Hanoi, but others, mostly hidden in the jungles of South Vietnam, were as far as 150 miles from Hanoi. Because POWs captured in South Vietnam would have to walk days to reach the North Vietnamese prisons, most were held in bamboo cages in the middle of the jungle. They experienced even worse conditions than prisoners in the North did.

To reach the prison camps in both the North and the South, the POWs and their guards traveled through villages. Often the peasants wanted to take part in punishing the POWs. The guards obliged. They forced the POWs to pass through a gauntlet, a narrow path flanked on each side by torturers. The angry peasants clubbed the POWs with anything at hand—sticks, gun butts, bamboo poles, or shovels. They pretended to jab the prisoners with pitchforks only to back off at the last minute when the VC officers would order them to stop. The guards had strict orders to deliver the soldiers to the prison camps alive. As a result, the guards sometimes sneaked their prisoners past villages to protect them from assaults.

While walking to the prison camps, the blindfolded soldiers usually wore a rope around the neck. Any time the prisoner strayed off the path or fell, a VC sol-

Hello Hanoi Hilton

Navy Captain William P. Lawrence remembers the day he got shot down on an early morning bombing raid in his F-4B Phantom. He said in the P.O.W. Network files (www. pownetwork.org):

I had been captured by a band of stick swinging peasants who turned me over to the armed citizenry. The militia decided that we should run the entire distance to the outpost where I would be transported to Hanoi. We ran two abreast with the peasants and tattered clothed children running along and poking and prodding me with sticks . . . after a two hour run, I was blindfolded, handcuffed and placed in a truck for the trip to Hanoi. There I was put on a floor and tied. In came the famous Bug . . . a professional jailer who went to work on me, literally stripping the flesh from my ankles with the leg irons. I still carry the cigarette burns on my arms, which are the result of a torture session.

As they were marched to prison camps, captured pilots suffered all forms of physical abuse.

dier tugged on the rope to pull the man along. If more than one prisoner was being moved at the same time, the VC shackled them with leg chains. During rest periods the prisoners were held in bamboo cages, placed in pits or tied to trees. During American bombing strikes, the POWs were shoved into bunkers or ditches along the trails.

Some of the POWs tried to escape before reaching the prison camps. Most managed to stay alive for a few days, hiding in the tall grass during the day and crawling through the jungle at night. Few escaped POWs managed to reunite with an American unit, however. Most were recaptured.

The Prison Camps

Most POWs were relieved when they finally reached the prison camps. They assumed that conditions in the prison would be better than they had been on the long journey through the jungle. They thought the food would be better in prison than it was on the road, and they expected to receive medical attention for their injuries. They also looked forward to seeing other Americans and talking with them. None of these hopes would come true. Lieutenant Com-

mander Robert Naughton remembered the disappointment:

The most profound effect of my early days of capture consisted of a realization that for the first time in my life I was completely on my own. All the training I had received was behind me now, and possibly for a long time. No one would come to my aid. When we found ourselves in trouble in America, we could count on being given the benefit of the doubt or a little kindness. Now, in prison, it was entirely up to me to perform and I could not expect any breaks.[8]

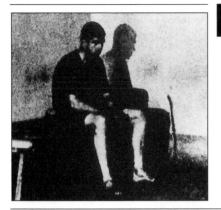

Chapter 2

Home Not-So-Sweet Home

Life in the Vietnam POW camps was unlike anything the American soldiers had encountered before. Nothing in their training fully prepared them for the isolation, starvation, and torture they would face. To survive, the POWs had to learn new skills and develop new resources within themselves. Even a strong will to survive did not guarantee success, however, because conditions in the prisons were unhealthy and even inhumane.

Depending on where they were captured, the POWs faced very different situations. POWs captured in Laos and South Vietnam were held in bamboo cages and specially constructed huts. Some of the bamboo huts were large and housed more than one man; others were small and made to hold only one person. To prevent escape, POWs in South Vietnam usually were chained and bound with ropes. The ropes were tied so tightly that the prisoners' hands and feet went numb. The ropes were eventually removed, but the chains remained. Some POWs were not removed from their cages for months at a time, and they had to lie in their own human waste. Captured in 1968, U.S. Army doctor Captain Floyd Kushner spent his time with eleven other prisoners in a number of campsites hidden in the forests near riverbeds. He said:

> From September to January six men died, most of them in my arms, and we—our ration was very low. We were eating approximately three coffee cups of vermin-infested rice a day, with some fish sauce. We had a terrible skin disease that was keeping people up all night. It was itching. It was causing a lot of psychological anguish as well as physical anguish. We were horribly malnourished. People had malaria and dysentery. . . . I don't know the words that can describe how bad these times were.[9]

The prisons in North Vietnam were nothing like those in the South. The North Vietnamese prisons had been built by the French at the turn of the century to imprison the Vietnamese during an earlier war. Though each camp had a Vietnamese name, the POWs quickly assigned their own American name to their camp. Camps in North Vietnam were dubbed Plantation, Zoo, Hanoi Hilton, Faith, Skidrow, Dogpatch, Alcatraz, Dirty Bird, Rockpile, Hope, Briarpatch, and Farnsworth.

The Zoo and Alcatraz, which were less exposed and less vulnerable to attack, housed senior officers and problem pris-

This Veterans Day parade in St. Louis, Missouri, shows some of the conditions POWs in Vietnam had to endure, such as being held in bamboo cages.

oners such as escapees. Torture was the most severe in these areas. Things were entirely different at the Plantation camp. Located in the former home of Hanoi's colonial mayor, the Plantation retained some of its former grandeur, which is how it got its nickname. The Plantation was reserved for new prisoners who had not yet been tortured. Thus, whenever representatives of the Red Cross or other humanitarian groups arrived in North Vietnam and were allowed to inspect prisons, the North Vietnamese took them to this prison.

First Days in Camp

Upon arriving in his assigned camp, the prisoner assessed his new home. The Hanoi Hilton, the primary facility, received the most prisoners and consisted of thick concrete walls fifteen to twenty feet high. At the top of the walls were a couple of feet of jagged broken bottles embedded in concrete and above that, several rows of barbed wire.

Just inside the main gate was a dry moat twenty feet in width. Machine gun-

ners on perches watched the prison perimeter at all times to prevent escapes. Inside, the prison compound was divided into interrogation rooms, offices, torture chambers, a courtyard, and four prison areas. The Americans gave each section of the prison a nickname: Heartbreak Hotel, Camp Unity, New Guy Village, and Little Vegas. Each prison block averaged about eight cells that were seven feet square. They were furnished with a cement or

The Hanoi Hilton, the infamous prison which held the majority of American POWs during the Vietnam War.

wooden slab bed with a set of rusted leg irons attached, a mosquito net, and a metal can, called a *bo*, to be used as a human waste bucket. Most cells had a high window that had been boarded up or covered with wire mesh. There was one dim lightbulb in the room.

In North Vietnamese prisons, the POWs were issued thin, khaki prison pajamas, a bar of soap, a thin cotton blanket, a toothbrush, a pair of tire-tread sandals, a drinking cup, and three pieces of toilet paper (expected to last ten days). During the early 1960s, inmates were kept in isolation much of the time and never allowed to see or communicate with other prisoners. They were taken out of their cells only oc-casionally for a bath or to go to the interrogation rooms for torture. They were issued three Vietnamese cigarettes a day. Those who did not smoke took the cigarettes anyway. Sometimes they gave their ration of cigarettes to their fellow inmates. Other times they used the cigarettes to bribe the guards into treating them better.

Interrogation

Within a few hours of his arrival at the prison camp, the POW was taken into a room to be interrogated to see what he knew about U.S. missions or troop locations. The majority of the POWs honored the Code of Conduct, which required that they resist their captors by all means open

Guards Varied in Temperament and Actions Toward the POWs

Every POW has stories about the varying treatment he received from the guards. Some guards hated the Americans and took out their anger and resentment on the prisoners every chance they got. Others were merely doing their jobs and remained detached from the treatment of the prisoners. Yet some behaved with basic human kindness, and POWs report times when the guards refused to inflict further torture, or times when a POW and his English-speaking guard passed time in conversations trying to learn each other's culture. Former POW Captain Thomas Moe said in an interview with the author:

> An army will not put its best people in prisons as guards. Their talents are needed elsewhere. Therefore, most of the guards were either rather dumb or were recovering from wounds, sometimes war wounds. . . .

Some of the guards were cruel as you would expect in any culture or country. They had absolute power over us and used it. They were restrained somewhat on a day-to-day basis, but when the authorities wanted us to get beat up, they would trot in the bad guys—and they loved it.

One guard and part-time translator was kind (although he was not a rocket scientist either). We called him "Mark," because of a mole he had on his temple. When he figured out what his nickname was, he was hurt and came to us for an explanation. One of my friends, truly not wanting to hurt Mark, told him that we called him "Mark," because it was one of the books of our Bible. Mark was relieved, and I was happy that my friend had thought of a kind explanation for a person that we all liked.

to them, and refused to give out any information other than their name, rank, and serial number. When they did not cooperate, they were tortured and beaten, often for more than fifteen hours at a time. Major George Day described his first interrogation in April 1968. Day's interrogator spoke broken English but made his actions clear by his rough manner and loud voice. Day recalled:

> They hung me up from the ceiling by ropes for hours which paralyzed my left hand for about a year and a half. I could barely move my right hand. My wrist curled up and my fingers were curling. I could just barely move my right thumb and forefinger. In some torture sessions, they were trying to make you surrender. The name of the game was to take as much brutality as you could until you got to the point that you could hardly control yourself and then surrender to their demands. The next day they'd start all over again.[10]

Early Release

Torture was not the only method the VC used to obtain information from POWs. Sometimes they tried to bribe the prisoners with the promise of freedom. Military protocol dictated that POWs would be released in the order of imprisonment, and word

went out that if anyone was offered early release, he must refuse unless he was mentally insane or had a serious health condition. The men knew the order in which each had become a prisoner and realized that if he violated the release order, he would be shunned by his comrades the rest of his life. The bond between most military personnel is so strong, this punishment was more feared than the brutality the VC handed out.

One prisoner who was tested with the offer to go home early was Lieutenant Commander John McCain, who later was

Senator John McCain visits the Hanoi Hilton in April 2000. As a POW, McCain never accepted offers of early release.

elected to the U.S. House of Representatives and the U.S. Senate. Captured in 1973, McCain was the son of Admiral John McCain II, soon to be the commander in chief of the Pacific fleet. The VC knew the captured pilot was an important man and offered him an early release. Although in poor physical health, the younger McCain never accepted the offers.

Camp Conditions

Camps did not have bathrooms. Some had a hole in the ground outside the cells in the prison compound where the POWs dumped their waste buckets once a day. At other camps, the buckets were collected by a POW and dumped in a designated spot. As the waste pile grew, so did its stench. Eventually, the pile would be removed or buried.

The extreme temperatures added to the POWs' discomfort. In summer, temperatures averaged one hundred degrees. The tin roofs on the cells magnified the heat. POWs had trouble breathing in the hot and humid weather and often had to lie on the floor by the crack under the door to catch a cool breath of air. The concrete block walls of the cells retained the heat so that even at night there was no relief. During these extreme temperatures, POWs perspired so profusely that any movement increased their discomfort. A simple walk to the latrine (toilet) was a monumental task. Water was scarce during summer, so the inmates would go for months without bathing.

During these times the POWs became very resourceful. One POW who was chained to his bed made a hole in the bed boards with his leg iron so he could urinate through the bed instead of wetting himself and having to lie in it.

In the winter months when the temperatures dipped to thirty degrees, the one thin blanket issued to the prisoners did little to keep them warm. Most of the men made it a practice to do several push-ups against the wall to get their blood circulating through their cold bodies every time they got out of bed.

All cells were rat infested. Having nothing else to do, some prisoners actually named the rodents and spent time counting them. Other visitors to the cells included spiders, geckos, roaches, mice, scorpions, and large ants. In some regions a *sing ha,* a black poisonous lizard about ten inches in length, sometimes crept into the cells. POWs had to be wary of this creature as its bite could kill.

Daily Routine

Each morning at 6 A.M., the prison guards woke the POWs by ringing a gong. Each man knew how important it was to stay mentally and physically active, so at this time he would begin his own exercise program in his cell or cage. At 10:30 A.M. the first meal of the day would be served. In mid-afternoon, another gong rang out, signaling the time for guards to partake in the Vietnamese custom of an afternoon nap. While the guards slept, the POWs took the

The Camp Rules

These Camp Regulations were posted inside most prison cells and are taken from *A POW's Story: 2801 Days in Hanoi.*

All U.S. aggressors caught red-handed in their piratical attacks against the Democratic Republic of Vietnam are criminals. While detained in this camp, you will strictly obey the following:

1. All criminals will bow to all officers, guards, and VC in the camp.

2. All criminals must show polite attitude at all times to the officers and guards in the camp, or they will be severely punished.

3. All criminals will answer any question orally or write any statement or do anything directed by the camp authority, or they will be severely punished.

4. Criminals are forbidden to attempt to communicate in any way, such as signals, tapping on the walls, attempting to communicate with criminals in the next room.

5. When in the bath area, do not attempt to communicate with criminals in the next area, or you will be severely punished.

6. Any criminal who attempts to escape, or help others to do so, will be severely punished.

7. On the other hand, criminals who follow these camp regulations and who show a good attitude by concrete acts will be shown a humane treatment.

signed: camp authority

---

opportunity to try to communicate with each other without risk of punishment. The second and last meal of the day was between 2:30 P.M. and 8:00 P.M., depending on the camp. Once a day, usually in the afternoon, prisoners were allowed to leave their cells to dump their waste bucket. In the evenings prisoners were taken to the interrogation rooms for torture. Bedtime was 9 P.M.

The VC allowed limited personal grooming. In some camps, the prisoners showered once every two weeks; in others, they went a month or more between showers. Military regulations required the American soldiers to shave, but the VC provided the POWs

with razors only once every two weeks. The POWs all used the same razor, which usually left their faces nicked and cut. Haircuts were rare and sometimes brutal as the VC barbers yanked at prisoners' hair and nicked them with the shears.

During the mid- to late-1960s, the VC realized the war was not ending as quickly as they had expected. As more Americans filled the prisons, the VC decided to use the prisoners to work around the camps. Although most POWs suffered from illness, they jumped at the opportunity to get out of their cells and perform tasks such as preparing food, doing dishes, and cleaning up.

One such task was given to Major Lawrence Guarino when a guard came to his cell and dumped a wheelbarrow of wet coal dust in the corner of his cell. Guarino was told to make balls of coal that would be used to cook food. Glad to have something to do, Guarino got busy. He enjoyed using not only his hands, but also his mind as he kept count of the balls he made—360 balls in all. When the guard returned, Guarino, covered head to toe with black coal dust, asked permission to wash. When the guard said no, Guarino lifted the top of his *bo* and pretended he was going to wash his hands in his own excrement. The guard yelled "No!" and led Guarino to the showers.

Passing Time

The prisoners had nothing in their cells or cages with which to occupy their minds. Bored and lonely, they were constantly looking for other ways to pass the time and keep their minds sharp. Locked in his bamboo cage for years in Laos, Ernest Brace was so bored he began to carve images on sandstones outside his cage with a piece of bamboo he sharpened on a rock. The images were so good the guards began to steal them so Brace put his name and date on them in case they made their way to fellow soldiers.

POWs spent many hours observing rodents and bugs. Ants provided hours of entertainment for the prisoners, who watched them drag food scraps to their nests. Rats infested the area and sometimes gave birth within the walls of the prison. Some POWs shared their food with the rats, mice, and even bugs in an attempt to make pets out of the wild creatures.

Unsavory Choices

The day's menu for soldiers varied but always contained some type of soup—pumpkin, cabbage, or rice—and a side dish of greens. Occasionally the men would receive a chunk of bread. The bread almost always contained rat droppings. Often the food was covered with dirt or contained chicken bones, animal hooves, rotten fish, or unidentifiable chunks of meat covered with animal hair.

Major Guarino once received a bowl of dirty rice garnished with a dog's skull. Guarino asked the guard why the cook served such slop. The guard said, "The cook wants you to know that he hates you."[11] Enraged at being served such a grotesque meal, Guarino went on a hunger strike, refusing to eat anything for the next forty-seven days.

At a few camps, cells had no lights, so the POWs who received their last daily meal in the evening often ate in darkness. Knowing that eating was one of the few pleasures the prisoners enjoyed, some guards tried to ruin the evening meal by allowing cockroaches to swarm over the POW's plate of food before shoving it under the door. Before he could eat, the prisoner had to brush the insects off the food and shake them off his arms and hands.

The food and water throughout the entire war were far below safe standards. At jungle camps in South Vietnam, the in-

You Had to Keep Busy

Discipline and activity were needed to fuel the minds and emotions of the prisoners. Doing something, anything, not only took their minds off of their despair, but provided energy and hope. Some prisoners practiced memorizing the names of other inmates so that they could tell military officials who else was in the prison, should they ever escape or be released. In an interview with the author, Commander James Stockdale said:

> You had to keep busy. You didn't just lie around and wait for them to ring the gong, you had a lot of things to do. Contrived things, but they filled the day. You had to have an exercise program, and that took about forty-five minutes. I did 400 push-ups a day, and it helped with my self-respect. Later I discovered it helped with my physical health for years to come. You had to go over your names. Each one of us kept an individual roster of names that eventually went over four hundred, and you recited these every day. If you forgot one, you went on the wall and asked your neighbor to give you his list for the letter in the group. You had a prayer period. And you did the same things at the same time every day.

Memorizing other prisoners' names was just one activity that kept POWs busy and focused on something other than their desperate situation.

mates sometimes drank water from rivers infested with parasites that gave the men dysentery (diarrhea). The mortality rate in these camps was especially high. The food also contained parasites. Captain Thomas Moe recalled in the P.O.W. Network files how he handled the food and water he was served. He said:

> Our drinking water smelled like the sewer water that it was—it would make you sick sometimes just to smell

it. I would let my cup of water sit for a few minutes just to let the sediment sink to the bottom. For years after I returned, I would never drink a glass of fluid until it was empty—so long was I accustomed to there being a residue at the bottom. The grassy watery weeds we were served for "soup" was served boiling hot in the summer and ice cold in the winter. The tin spoons we ate with would rasp along the bottom of the bowl because of the sediment (sand, pebbles, wire . . .). Rat droppings infested the bread like dark little balls of chocolate. We would pick out the rat droppings so that the pieces of bread looked like Swiss cheese and eat what was left. The wire, razor blades, etc. in the soup simply found their way there because our captors had no sense of hygiene.[12]

Food became such an obsession for the POWs that the guards marveled at how the prisoners could spend hours eating one meal. Little crumbs of bread were lingered over and then devoured as if they were special treats. When they were not playing with their food, they were dreaming about it. Lieutenant Commander Robert Doremus explained:

Eating even the meager rations was something to do. But, instead of eating it all, you'd take half of it and decide how you were going to eat the rest. You could even make a sandwich out of rice, roll it in a ball, and divide it. You'd take half an hour playing with it before you'd even eat it. Then, you'd chew it very slowly watching for the rocks in it. The Vietnamese couldn't believe the way we played around with our food. You could string the whole thing out to about an hour-and-a-half. And that's an hour-and-a half of your time that's gone.

I daydreamed (and night-dreamed) of menus and methods of preparation, until I thought I had eaten the very food I conjectured. . . . For a period of about a year my roommate and I would pass our recommended breakfast menu . . . complete with the wine or booze of the day . . . in a coded message to a solo in the next cell. . . . We could conjure visions of anything from grits and red-eyed gravy to six different styles of cheesecake. I could spend a happy, busy, and interesting hour "on the wall" learning about someone's grandmother's recipe for mince meat pie.[13]

Mental and Physical Health Care

Health care for the POWs was as poor as the food choices. The unsanitary food made the POWs prone to infections and parasites. Some removed worms longer than six inches from their throats. Whenever possible the POWs tried to locate peppers growing wild and eat them, claiming they helped keep the worms away. If they happened to

All types of parasitic worms infected POWs because of the unsanitary conditions in which the prisoners were kept.

themselves. Prisoners who shared cells were better off because their cell mates could administer aid. When prisoners returned from beatings, their cell mates massaged their hands for hours to restore circulation.

A properly treated insect or snakebite does not pose a major danger to a healthy person, but for the malnourished POWs, venomous bites that went untreated sometimes resulted in death.

In the beginning of the war, prisoners were given some medical treatment, but as time went on the VC treated their captives more harshly. At first, new prisoners received injections of quinine and penicillin to ward off infections, but as the war went on and supplies of drugs dwindled, the VC gave fewer injections to the captives. Often, the VC provided medical care only to prisoners who cooperated with prison authorities.

Taking care of their physical needs became a full-time job for those who hoped to survive their imprisonment.

be in a room where there was a kerosene lantern, they would steal a quick drink of the kerosene, again in hopes of killing parasites in their body. When they extracted their own teeth, they packed the hole with tobacco, hoping the nicotine in the roasted leaves would lessen the ache.

Broken bones and fractures went untreated and often were set by the POWs

Chapter 3

Communication: A Key to Survival and Resistance

To keep their prison camps secure, limit the number of attempted escapes, and prevent prisoner unrest, VC prison officials knew they had to keep American POWs from communicating with one another. Individual attempts to resist control posed no serious danger to the camp, but well-organized and well-coordinated resistance could. As a result, the VC posted regulations in most prison cells that strictly forbade communication between prisoners in any way, such as signals, tapping on walls, or trying to talk to prisoners in adjoining rooms. Those who broke this rule risked torture and even death.

American POWs tried to communicate despite this rule. Their own Code of Conduct required that they resist their captors "by all means necessary." The Code of Conduct also called for senior officers to take command in prison, which required communication. To prevent the enemy from realizing that communication was taking place and to avoid punishment, the POWs did not attempt to communicate openly by shouting or even speaking aloud. Rather, they devised secret forms of communication. Some of the techniques were simple, such as passing notes. Others were more elaborate and sometimes even bizarre.

Establishing Command

The senior officer of each camp was expected to take the leadership and assume control of the men, just as he would have in combat. The duties of the senior officer included learning the names and ranks of fellow prisoners, finding out what camps they had been held in, and determining their physical condition. He was responsible for making sure his men followed the Code of Conduct established by President Dwight Eisenhower in 1955. The senior officers planned and coordinated tactics, operated an effective organization, and sustained morale.

To prevent the VC from knowing who the senior officers were, the POWs made up code names for the officers. The names only remained in effect for a short time because the VC often learned who the senior officers were either by reading American newspapers and magazines or by torturing POWs until they gave up information. Once discovered, the senior officers usu-ally were isolated from the other prisoners. Even then, the senior officers found ways to continue to lead, finding secret hiding places to leave notes or learning how to use simple objects to communicate.

Tools Used to Communicate

Even though POWs could expect punish-ment if they attempted to communicate, most of them took the risk to talk or write to a fellow prisoner. To communicate, the prisoners used all sorts of utensils. For ex-ample, if a prisoner was left in the interro-gation room alone, even for a moment, he would steal a pencil for later use. Because the cells were frequently inspected, prison-ers sometimes hid their pencils in the la-trine. Later, a prisoner who visited the latrine to shave could use the razor to cut up the pencil. The cut-up pieces of pencil lead were easy to hide and distribute to other prisoners. Equipped with the lead, prisoners could write messages on toilet pa-per or unrolled cigarette paper. In one in-cident, fearing torture when a cell-to-cell search for contraband began, two cell mates broke their pencil in half and chewed it up.

Prisoners who did not have pencils or lead sometimes made pens from the bam-boo plants that grew outside their windows. The POWs broke the bamboo shoots into strips and dipped the end into ink made from a mixture of cigarette ashes and wa-ter. Other prisoners used toothpaste to make a crude ink. Some POWs even learned to make a kind of grease pencil out

---

Implementing the Operation Plan

When Commander Jeremiah Denton was moved to the Zoo, he immediately used the pencil he had stolen at the Hanoi Hilton to write an operation plan. When given the usual cough or all-clear notice that no guards were in the area, he read his plan aloud for the POWs to hear. The plan contained the following:

1. Follow the Code of Conduct.

2. Communicate by all means available.

3. Don't try to escape without outside help.

4. Don't antagonize the guards.

5. Learn all POW names and locations (each building number and room num-ber to be included).

6. Collect and save matches, wire, nails, rope, and paper.

7. Complain about the food, clothing, no exercise or church services.

8. Church services on Sunday will be sig-naled by whistling "God Bless America."

9. Maintain a listening watch. Sleep when the VC sleeps.

of bread, soap, and charcoal. These ingenious prisoners would dampen a piece of bread, roll it around a wire, and leave it to dry. When the bread had hardened, the prisoner would remove the wire, leaving a hollow core. He would then fill the core with a mixture of charcoal and soap that he had softened by rolling it in his hands. By forcing the dark, greasy mixture to the tip of the pencil, the prisoner could write with it.

Passing notes was even more difficult than writing them. When possible, the men dug holes under their walls to pass notes to the man in the next cell. POWs at one camp devised a way to leave messages in the shower area. They placed their notes in an old bottle that was hidden from view behind a small concrete slab. The author of the note would then bend a wire that dangled from the sink in a certain way that let other prisoners know that a new note had been left.

Those who did not have paper sometimes used their spoons to scratch notes on the bottom of their tin plates, hoping that POWs on cleanup detail might be able to read their words. Of course, the guards might discover the messages as well, but sometimes the men were so desperate to communicate that the idea of another POW reading the message outweighed the risk of punishment.

Whenever a POW had an urgent message he wished to convey, he might risk talking through the wall. Covering his head with his blanket to muffle the sound of his

Messages Were Found Everywhere

U.S. Air Force Major Guarino was incarcerated in the Hanoi Hilton in June 1965 and not released until 1973. During one of his first days in prison, he was returned to his cell and noticed something strange on the wall. He writes in *A POW's Story: 2801 Days in Hanoi:*

As I sat on the edge of the steel cot, my eyes fell upon something written on the cell wall directly in front of me. I leaned over, my heart gave a leap as I read the words "Look under table." What table? There was no table here; it must mean under the bench with the leg stocks. I scurried over, dropped to my knees, and checked out the underside of the rack, but found nothing. Maybe there was a table and it had been removed from the cell? Frustrated, I sat down again, but every few minutes I got up and checked the bench. Suddenly I got an idea. Picking up the small stool in the corner, I looked carefully at the top. Scratched into the grain faintly with a pencil was "look under." I quickly flipped the stool over. There stuffed into a crack of the wood, was a tightly folded note. Turning my back to the door, I picked up the toilet bucket and held it in front of me as a fake in case the guard peeked in. "Hi," I read. "About six weeks here before move. Food pretty good. No torture. You will be contacted. Keep your eyes and ears open. Pray and put your trust in God. Yank."

voice, the speaker would place his tin drinking cup against the wall, place his lips inside the cup, and speak. The cup acted as a megaphone, preventing sound waves from escaping to the sides and directing them to the wall.

A few resourceful POWs made dime-sized holes in their cell walls through which to talk. They drilled the holes by removing the wire handles from their water buckets and twisting the ends of the handle against the concrete. To prevent the guards from knowing what they were doing, the prisoners hid the holes by stuffing bits of bread or other matter into the holes. The men knew that if the holes were discovered, both they and the prisoners in the next cell would be beaten, but they thought the risk was worth it.

At some camps the bath areas were divided into several stalls connected by one drainpipe. POWs would lift the trap and speak to the guy in the next stall for brief amounts of time. At the Zoo, where approximately eighty-five prisoners were held, the camp latrine was located next to a prison cell. Each time a POW walked

POWs shower while under guard. In some camps bath areas were divided into stalls, allowing prisoners to communicate briefly.

past the cell on the way to empty his bucket, he quietly exchanged a sentence or two with whoever was being held in the cell at the time.

Passing notes, scratching messages into tin plates, and drilling holes in the walls all left behind evidence of communication that could lead to punishment. Even speaking through the walls with a tin cup was dangerous. To avoid detection, the POWs needed a form of communication that left no trail and did not attract attention. Air force Captain Carlyle Harris offered one solution. He remembered a code system he had learned in survival training that used a system of taps or knocks. The tap code was similar to the more common Morse code, but it was easier to learn. Harris introduced the tap code to fellow POWs in 1965, and it quickly became the most commonly used method of communication throughout the prison system.

The Tap Code

The code was instituted immediately by POWs and taught to new prisoners as soon as they came into the system. It became their second language. To start a communication, the POW tapped the rhythm for "shave and a haircut" on the wall. If the answer of "two bits" came back, the communication continued. Each letter of the alphabet could be expressed by a unique series of taps. Slowly the prisoners spelled out words and sentences.

To save time, the POWs developed a kind of shorthand, spelling out parts of words or abbreviations instead of full words. For example, the letters QZ stood for *quiz*, which meant interrogation. The letters QZR meant *quizzer*, or interrogator. If the receiver of the message knew what word was being sent, he would give two quick taps. The sender would then skip to the next word. POWs who were imprisoned for a long time eventually learned to recognize the individual style, or "hand," of the tapper.

Most of the tapping would be done at noon when the guards were having their lunch, in the afternoons when the guards napped, or at night. A POW who had a window facing the entryways would make a noise to let everyone know it was okay to tap, or cough to let everyone know someone was coming. At one camp the POWs whistled "Pop Goes the Weasel" as a warning to stop tapping, and "Mary Had a Little Lamb," as an all clear. With the aid of the lookouts, men could communicate around the clock.

As the tap code became ingrained in the prisoners' minds, they began to think of new ways to send messages. When the POWs were sweeping, for example, they would stroke the broom so that the swishing sounds spelled out letters in tap code. Likewise, when the inmates used a wire brush to clean out their waste buckets, they would swish the brush in code. Some inmates would cough, snort, or clear their throats in tap code. When bathing or washing their clothes, the POWs sometimes snapped their wet clothes in tap code.

The prisoners even figured out how to use the code to communicate without making any sounds at all. For example, when Commander Stockdale was placed in solitary confinement, he unraveled threads from his clothes and tied tiny knots in them at different intervals. Another prisoner could read these "braille messages" by holding the thread lightly between two fingers and pulling the end of the thread at a uniform rate. Each knot could be read as a tap.

Silent messages could also be sent by sight. A prisoner with a window could hold up his fingers, the end of his toothbrush, or some other object for a moment to signify a tap. The same technique could be used in cracks or under doors. The prisoners could flash a piece of toilet paper or other thin object through the crevice in code.

In a world absent of family and friends, the POWs had to sustain each other emotionally. They tapped messages about their families. They shared stories and jokes. Some POWs maintained that a joke tapped to them after they returned from a beating actually may have saved their lives. The prisoners even learned to detect mood changes through the tapping system. "We became sensitive to the range of acoustic perception," said Stockdale. "We could actually decipher a guy's mood by tapping. It's the touch. It came out like the tone of voice. The way he emphasized things, you knew if he was down in the dumps or happy."[14]

New prisoners were sometimes wary of attempts made to communicate with them.

The Tap Code

The tap code was the principal means POWs used to communicate. POWs who did not know the code needed a written copy of the letter scheme at first either on paper or scratched somewhere in their cell. Eventually they all memorized the order of the letters in their head. To use the code, the sender would tap first to denote the row; the second set of taps denoted the column. Each letter required two sets of taps. For example, for the letter S, four taps, a pause, then three taps meant row four, column three.

		Columns				
		1	2	3	4	5
Rows	1	A	B	C	D	E
	2	F	G	H	I	J
	3	L	M	N	O	P
	4	Q	R	S	T	U
	5	V	W	X	Y	Z

Lieutenant Commander John McCain remembered that a former marine named Ernie Brace was particularly difficult to contact. Brace had been captured while flying in supplies for the U.S. Agency for International Development and military units of the CIA. Brace was imprisoned in a bamboo cage and bound in ropes and leg irons for three years. He attempted three escapes and was tortured severely each time. After one attempt, he was placed in a pit in the ground and buried up to his chin. For a week, Brace was unable to move his body, even while the bugs crawled over his face. In 1968, Brace was brought to the Hanoi Hilton and placed in a cell next to McCain. McCain writes:

I tried to tap him up on the wall. In terrible shape, and fearful that the knocks he heard in the cell next door were made by Vietnamese trying to entrap him in an attempted violation of the prohibition against communicating, he made no response. For days I tried in vain to talk to him. Finally, he tapped back, a faint but audible "two bits." I put my drinking cup to the wall. . . . "Do you have a drinking cup." No response . . . his suspicion of being set up by the Vietnamese intensified as I urged him to make illicit use of it.

A few days later, the possibility that he could talk with another American for the first time in three years overrode his understandable caution. . . . To my query, Ernie would only manage to say his name before he broke down. I could hear him crying. After his long, awful years in the jungle, the sound of an American voice, carrying with it the promise of fraternity with men who would share his struggle, had overwhelmed him.[15]

Letters to and from Home

Communication from the world outside the prison was as important as communication inside. For the first few years of the war, the POWs were not permitted to send or receive mail except during the Christmas and Easter seasons. Those who did get to send or receive letters soon learned that

there was always a catch. The POWs were told to write their return address as "To U.S. Criminals Caught Red-Handed." When they refused, they were allowed to inscribe "Camp of Detention of U.S. Pilots Captured in the Democratic Republic of Vietnam" instead. Eventually some POWs were allowed to write letters home. POWs who had gained a name for themselves,

A mother holds up a picture of her son who is a POW. Some prisoners were eventually allowed to write letters home.

were known in the media, or were of high rank were allowed to write. Others were not. While this concept violated the rules of the Code of Conduct, the senior officers decided that prisoners who had permission to write should do so, the goal being to get as much information out as possible about the prisoners.

The prisoners had to be careful about what they put in the letters. All letters that traveled in and out of the prison system, even those sent by the Red Cross, were read by the Vietnamese Committee for Liaison. Prisoners often lied about their treatment just so the Vietnamese would allow the letters to be sent.

Once the prisoners realized that their families were actually receiving their mail, they began to place secret messages within the letters. A POW might insert the name, nickname, or initials of a fellow prisoner into the letter, pretending it was the name of a friend or relative. These messages were not always understood at first. For example, Marlene McGrath was confused by a letter she received from her husband, Lieutenant Mike McGrath, because he called their son John "J. J." Later she discovered that he was trying to tell her about someone in the camp.

The prisoners knew that the American military read all the letters families received, so they sometimes encrypted their messages, using a secret code that the military might decipher. Sometimes they wrote words a little higher than oth-

ers in the sentence. When all of the raised words were put together, they revealed a secret message. Some men placed dots above certain letters to spell out messages.

The families of POWs and the military also sent secret messages to the POWs. Stockdale did not know what to make of a letter he received from his wife Sybil that contained a picture of a woman he did not know but was labeled with the name of his mother. Knowing the woman was not his mother, Stockdale began to look for hidden clues in the photo or some type of secret message. Finding none, he finally placed the photo in a liquid mixture of tea and urine to make the photographic layers separate and discovered instructions from the navy written in invisible carbon. The message told him how to encrypt a letter home. To alert his wife that the letter was coded and should be sent to the navy for deciphering, Stockdale was told to address the letter to "Darling."

McCain also received a secret message from the navy. Chewing on a soft piece of candy that came in a package from home, McCain suddenly heard a crunch. He had bitten into a plastic capsule hidden inside the candy. Inside the capsule was a tiny note from the navy. The note told McCain the liner of the candy tin contained invisible ink. He was instructed to use the liner to write invisible messages in his letters home. McCain was never allowed to write a letter without Vietnamese supervision, so he never got to use the liner.

By 1969 packages from home began to arrive with various items inside. Anyone wanting his package had to sign a form stating "Due to the humane policy of the DRV, I received this package from home."

At first the prisoners complied, but as time went by this practice irritated them, and they refused the packages. The senior officers told the others to accept the packages, however, and to enjoy the con-

The Code of Conduct

As a result of tactics used by the Communists during the Korean War to brainwash prisoners, the Code of Conduct for all members of the U.S. military, taken from an Internet government site, was established as follows:

1. I am an American fighting man. I serve in the forces which guard my country and our way of life. I am prepared to give my life in their defense.

2. I will never surrender of my own free will. If in command, I will never surrender my men while they still have the means to resist.

3. If I am captured I will continue to resist by all means available. I will make every effort to escape and aid others to escape. I will accept neither parole nor special favors from the enemy.

4. If I become a prisoner of war, I will keep faith with my fellow prisoners. I will give no information or take part in any action which might be harmful to my comrades. If I am senior, I will take command. If not, I will obey the lawful orders of those appointed over me and will back them up in every way.

5. When questioned, should I become a prisoner of war, I am bound to give only name, rank, service number, and date of birth. I will evade answering further questions to the utmost of my ability. I will make no oral or written statements disloyal to my country and its allies or harmful to their cause.

6. I will never forget that I am an American fighting man, responsible for my actions and dedicated to the principles which made my country free. I will trust in my God and in the United States of America.

An American flight nurse helps feed a freed POW in Korea. Because of the Communist brainwashing tactics used during the Korean War, the Code of Conduct was established.

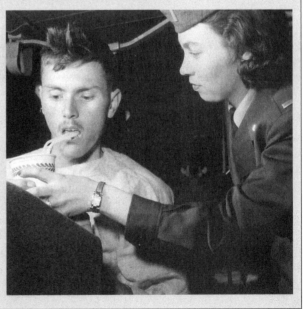

tents that were not pilfered by the guards and share with those who got nothing. The men received underclothes, toothbrushes, and toothpaste. Some prisoners were so hungry that they sometimes ate the toothpaste. The prisoners saved some items, such as chewing gum, to trade with the guards for information or better treatment. The guards always removed American cigarettes, which they traded on the black market.

After 1971, more packages arrived from home and some contraband began to get through. One man received cakes with rolls of microfilm that contained news of home, which he read by moonlight to his cell mates. When the guards discovered this trick, they began cutting every ounce of food into shreds before they gave it to the prisoners. Some packages held weapons, such as makeshift knives. The government started sending in parts of a radio. Almost immediately after the radio was assembled, it was discovered and confiscated.

Sometimes not receiving mail was as significant as receiving it. Sometimes a POW stopped receiving letters because a parent or spouse was gravely ill or had died. In some cases, wives of POWs who could not endure the separation filed for divorce in the soldiers' absence. When the mail stopped arriving, the POW was left wondering why. He usually would not learn the answer until he was released and returned home.

With little or no contact with loved ones back home, communication with fellow POWs literally became a matter of survival. Writing notes, speaking through walls, or tapping out code while the guards slept, the POWs supported each other emotionally. Soldiers fighting together in war have always formed a special bond, but because of the harsh conditions the POWs faced in Vietnam, their bond became even stronger.

Chapter 4

Torture and Isolation

Information is vital during time of war. Military leaders base their strategies on their knowledge of the position, strength, and armament of enemy troops. Advance information about enemy plans can give military leaders time to create effective countermeasures and thwart attacks. Such information can be obtained by a variety of methods, including eavesdropping on radio communications, placing spies behind enemy lines, and convincing enemy forces to commit treason and reveal secret information. Captured enemy soldiers also can be good sources of information, but few soldiers are willing to betray their comrades by providing the enemy with information. To force captured soldiers to divulge secrets, captors sometimes resort to mental coercion or physical torture.

Like captives in other wars, POWs in Vietnam were tortured to obtain information. The guards also tortured prisoners to reinforce who was in control of the camps

and break the prisoners' will to resist. Sometimes they tortured the POWs for propaganda purposes—to obtain false confessions of alleged war crimes or false statements about humane conditions in the camps. The guards also resorted to torture to convince the soldiers that the Communist philosophy was the correct method of government. During their first few weeks in prison the POWs underwent hours of indoctrination with lectures about Vietnamese history, Communism, and the evils of capitalism. The Communists believed that if they could convince the Americans that they had been fighting for the wrong ideas, the prisoners would be humble and less resistant to control.

At first the guards tried to coerce the prisoners through verbal abuse, psychological pressure, or denying food, toothbrushes, or bathing privileges. Air force Major James Kasler, a pilot shot down in August 1966, described the coercion techniques used on him and others:

Former POW Jeremiah Denton shows how he was tortured while a prisoner in Vietnam.

ture it remains vivid in his memory for months. Brainwashing has been described as torture, fear, relief, and then repeated until the individual becomes receptive to and is willing to parrot anything he is told. Isolation, starvation and denial of sleep are used in conjunction with brainwashing to reduce an individual's resistance. The Vietnamese employed all of these techniques but they were crude and ruthless in their approach. They were impatient for results and when they were not forthcoming, they became even more ruthless.[16]

The guards usually followed the same order of interrogation. First the interrogators asked for military information—rank, assignments, what the men knew about operations. They wanted to know what kind of planes the men flew, what kind of weapons were on board, and areas targeted for operations. Next were questions about the soldier's family. These were followed by political questions about the United States, including any personal relationships the soldier might have with high-ranking military officers or politicians. Some POWs had relatives or close friends who were officers in the military or members of Congress. The guards wanted to tread lightly with these prisoners

The Vietnamese kept us in isolation and denied us anything to occupy our minds for a good reason; for when a man living under these conditions is subjected to any mental inputs or torin fear of future retaliation. In some cases, especially with longtime prisoners, the guards demanded inside information about other prisoners. The interrogators wanted to know who was in command inside the camp so they could isolate the leaders or move them to other camps.

Creating Memories That Last

Lieutenant Mike McGrath was severely injured while ejecting from his plane. He suffered a broken and dislocated arm and fractured vertebrae and knee. The brutal torture sessions that followed resulted in additional injuries. His other shoulder and elbow were dislocated, and he was denied medical treatment. Alone in his cell for a year, McGrath had to find a way to survive not only physically but also mentally. Although gruesome, his method of survival eventually turned into an art form, and when he was released from prison McGrath became an illustrator for many of the books that the POWs wrote about their years in captivity. On the P.O.W. Network website (www.pownetwork.org) he describes how he became an artist:

> For a year I just laid on the floor trying to make my parts move. Finally I got a hold of the windowsill and relocated my own elbow and got my shoulder straight and started a long healing process. I couldn't sleep and my mind was in delirium. I started squeezing pus and blood out of my boils and painted a big beautiful stag horn sheep with a big set of horns on the wall. Over the years I'd memorize everything I saw and commit pictures to mind with the intent of drawing it one day when I got out.

POWs Expected Torture

The POWs in Vietnam knew they would be tortured. For the first two to four weeks after arriving in a camp, the guards pulled the POWs from their cells and led them "out to quiz," as the POWs called the interrogation sessions.

The interrogators quickly learned the prisoners would not give up information willingly. Before the violent torture began, the POW had to be worn down. The guards made the prisoner sit on a stool and ordered him not to move. They would keep the prisoner on the stool for up to ten days with only brief breaks for visiting the latrine. If the prisoner moved, the guards would beat him. Although "stool time" seemed torturous, worse things lay ahead.

Physical Torture

After the POW was worn down, the torturer was brought in, usually wearing boots. The first thing the torturer would do was kick the prisoner in the back. This first blow often caused internal injuries. The torturer would seemingly lose control, slapping, kicking, and screaming at the prisoner. After the savage beating, the torturer would leave the room for a short time, only to return with a new method of torture.

After the initial beating, the guards would force the POW to lie on the ground, then tie his arms behind his back. The torturer would then pull on the rope, forcing the prisoner's arms back so far that the shoulders often became dislocated. In this position, breathing became labored and

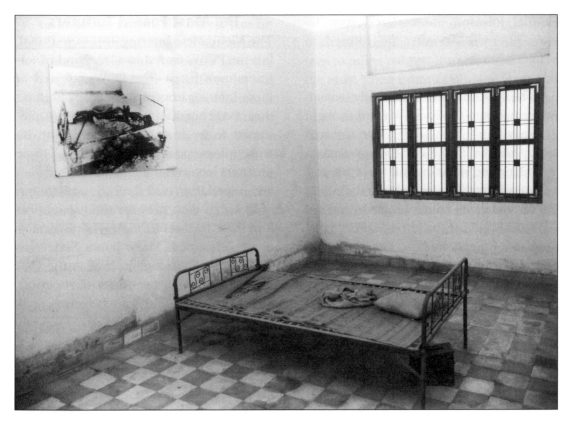

This photograph shows a room used by the North Vietnamese to torture American POWs.

the pain was intense. If the POWs cried out, the guards stuffed dirty rags into their mouths. Sometimes the torturers hung the prisoner from the ceiling on a hook, giving the torturer better leverage to pull the prisoner's arms back. Some prisoners were left to hang for days from these hooks.

After being caught communicating with another POW in 1972, Lieutenant Commander Theodore Guy was bound by ropes and forced to kneel for so long that his knees became the size of basketballs. The guards beat Guy with a rubber hose for ten days and nights, causing his skin to become raw and bloody and giving him a

double hernia. Guy asked the guards to kill him, but they only laughed. Finally they returned him to his cell.

Most prison guards were men, but many Vietnamese women served in the military and worked as guards. Some even made visits to the interrogation rooms. The women hated the Americans as intensely as their male counterparts did and acted just as brutally. Major

his lungs. The guards kept up the procedure until the prisoner's lungs nearly filled with water, stopping only moments before the prisoner would have drowned. Starved for air, the prisoner would cough violently, trying to expel water from his lungs. Water torture caused intense pain in the lungs and left the prisoner exhausted.

When a prisoner was uncooperative, the Vietnamese would put him into the "black box," a short hole in the ground inhabited by an anthill. A wooden door would be closed over the prisoner's head, forcing him to squat. Unable to move in the confined space, the prisoner would be bitten repeatedly by the ants, causing intense pain.

Even the thought of torture was torture. Major John Fer said, "The worst thing in prison was hearing the guard's keys rattle as he walked the halls and then hearing him rattle the cell doors at night. He could have been coming to take you for a torture session."[20]

After one escape attempt at the Zoo and many days of torture, Major Lawrence Guarino said in *A POW's Story: 2801 Days in Hanoi* that he was forced to admit he was the senior officer of the camp and had passed a message by tap code. The guards punished him by blindfolding him, placing him in leg irons, and forcing him to kneel

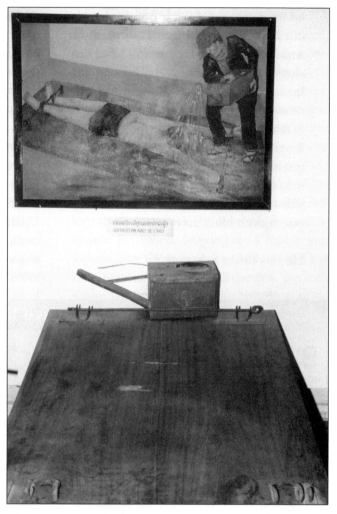

Pictured is a water-torture table. Water torture was one of the many forms of physical abuse inflicted on POWs.

from 6 A.M. until 6 P.M., causing his knees to swell and ache. If he tried to rise, the guards beat him. They alternated tying his hands, wiring his thumbs together, and making him extend his arms overhead. At night he was allowed to sit on a stool but never to sleep. When Guarino heard his fellow prisoners being brutally beaten in the next cell, he broke a glass window to attract the guards' attention. He then tried to slash his wrist on the broken glass to further distract the guards. His plan worked. The guards stopped punching the other inmates, but they hanged Guarino by his neck from a tree the next day, letting him down just before he suffocated.

A POW could receive torture for a simple act of kindness. When Lieutenant Commander Paul Gallant received a package from home, he wanted to share the contents with fellow prisoners. He threw a package of candy to another cell, and a guard saw it. As punishment Gallant was made to sit on a small stool in the interrogation room during the coldest season of the year for ten days and nights with no sleep.

In the beginning years of the POWs' captivity, the guards often withheld water as a form of punishment. When Colonel Robinson Risner was rushed to the hospital with kidney stones, the practice was eliminated and POWs then received unlimited water. Risner recalled his treatment and writes:

I was lying on my stomach groaning with pain. . . . The doctor raised his fist and hit me a sharp blow right over the kidney.

The last thing I remembered was pain so intense that I passed out. When I came to, I was vomiting and choking. No one would help me. . . . They re-fused to use the stretcher to carry me in. I began inching my way out. On my hands, knees and stomach, I crawled to the door of the hospital.

. . . They brusquely lifted me up and again we waited for a medic or doctor. Finally someone dressed in white came, either a medic or an intern, thumped my back and decided on a treatment.

It was a long needle into my kidney through my back, and then a couple of injections through the needle.

. . . I was in pain for days and days. They gave me medicine orally to ease that.[21]

The guards also used hunger and food to torture inmates. When Risner was in solitary and had been without food for several days, the guard finally brought him a piece of bread and a cup of water. As Risner reached for the bread it was knocked out of his hands to the ground. As Risner reached for it the second time, the guard clobbered him again. Risner writes: "I discovered that I could eat only on his command, like a dog. He would say, 'Okay,' I would pick it up, take a bite, and he would motion for me to put it back. Then I would have to wait at his whim before I could eat another bite. When I finally finished eating the bread, I asked for the water. He poured it out and took the cup with him."[22]

POWs Resisted Being Put on TV for Propaganda

Some of the worst tortures resulted when the guards attempted to get the POWs ready for TV cameras to show the world media how well they were treated. In order not to send a false message back to the United States, the POWs would do anything to keep this from happening, even hurt themselves. Major James Helms Kasler recalled his experience in the P.O.W. Network files (www.pownetwork.org). He writes:

> My worst session of torture began in late June 1968. The Vietnamese were attempting to force me to meet a delegation and appear before TV cameras on the occasion of the supposed 30,000th American airplane over North Vietnam. I couldn't say the things they were trying to force me to say. I was tortured for six weeks. I went through the rope and iron torture ten times. I was denied sleep for five days and during three of these was beaten every hour on the hour with a fan belt.

During the entire period I was on a starvation diet. I was very sick. In 1967 I contracted osteomyelitis, a massive bone infection in my right leg. They wrapped each leg before each torture session so I wouldn't get pus or blood all over the floor of the interrogation room. During this time they beat my face to a pulp. I couldn't get my teeth apart for five days. My eardrum was ruptured, one of my ribs broken, and a pin in my right leg was broken loose and driven up into my hip.

I surrendered a number of times during this torture session, but when they tried to get me to do something, I would refuse. By the time they were finished with me, I was in no condition to do anything. I lay in agony for six months until I was given an operation by the camp surgeon in January of 1969.

Many POWs were tortured in order to get them to appear before members of the media.

Mental and Psychological Torture

The guards also tortured the POWs in various ways to wear them down emotionally. When prisoners became disoriented, the guards often preyed upon their confusion. After his capture and before he was put into prison, Johnson saw a man wearing a Red Cross emblem approach him. Johnson thought he was going to get the medical treatment he needed, and his spirits lifted. But when the man presented Johnson with a pen and paper, even though Johnson's arm was so badly damaged he could not hold the pen, and asked him to write a letter saying how well and humanely he had been treated, Johnson understood. He writes in his book *Captive Warriors:*

> As an arm of a communist government, the Red Cross in North Vietnam was operated by the military, and it responded to prisoners of war under the direction of the military. But more importantly, it operated under the direction of the communist party. What I had yet to learn was that there was no freedom within the ranks to think or respond with compassion. Communist doctrine permeates every military organization, down to the lowest level, and controls all the actions of the military, including the Red Cross. Later I would see that a party member actually held more power than a high-ranking military commander. Party position always took priority over military rank.[23]

Sometimes the guards showed lower-ranking POWs confessions supposedly signed by high-ranking officers, hoping that after seeing the phony confession, the POWs would be persuaded to give up more information. Most POWs never fell for the trick.

During the years in the cells, the men were subjected to daily doses of what they called the "Box," radio programs broadcast in English that presented distorted views of the war. The Voice of Vietnam radio programs presented the POWs with false statements about how many American planes were shot down, or how Americans were losing interest in the war. The Communists hoped the reports would break the morale of the POWs, causing them to reconsider their allegiance and even agree to sign confessions. Johnson recalls one such message:

> Lay down your arms! Refuse to fight! Demand to be taken home, now! Today! Do you want to die in a foreign land, twelve thousand miles from your home? The American criminals have bombed Vietnam's dikes and dams and flooded the country. They are killing innocent women and children. Our food supplies are destroyed, our crops wiped out. You will pay for the crimes of your countrymen.[24]

The Vietnamese may have thought that the constant barrage of propaganda would weaken the POWs' spirit, but in many cases it had the opposite effect. Reports on the radio that described the Americans as cowards did not cause the POWs to give up. These attacks angered the troops, causing them to resist even more. Lieutenant Tom McNish said, "I had an undying faith that my country was not going to forget me no matter how long I stayed there or no matter if I died there, my country was not going to forget me. I was vital and that helped sustain me. I knew as long as I stayed alive I was going to get back."[25]

The Communists also tried to weaken the POWs' allegiance to their country by showing them mutilated bodies of women and children and stating that the Americans were to blame for the atrocities. They showed photos of American riots and protests and told the POWs that Americans no longer cared about them or the war.

Immediately after his capture Commander Stockdale met Nguyen Khac Vien, a North Vietnamese propaganda expert. Stockdale said:

Vien told me, "Americans know about the war as a matter of weapons, and the Vietnamese people know we cannot compete with you on the battlefield. But it's not that that wins wars anyway. It's a matter of natural will and when the American people get an idea of what this war is about, they will lose interest in pursuing it. We are going to win this war on the streets of New York, and when the American people understand this war, and you

and your fellow prisoners will help them understand it—you will be their teachers—then the war will go away."[26]

Risner described one ploy that disturbed him more than the physical torture he endured. He writes that a woman guard called Dragon Doll "was so mean that she would harangue the women convicts until they cried." On one occasion,

When the military guards brought me in, she opened the cell door and stood glaring all the time.

. . . It was not long before Dragon Doll brought in a little boy about five years old. He was of course too short to reach up to the peephole in the door. She lifted him up and said something to him. He would go, "Shush! Shush!," as they do with an animal, and then she would take his fist and shake it at me. That hurt me so bad I could hardly stand it, for he was one of the first children I had seen in weeks.[27]

Daily humiliation was a form of mental torture. Some guards visited some prisoners' cells many times a day to make the captives bow to them, knowing that this outraged the proud soldiers. In hot summer weather, guards sometimes led POWs to the showers only to reveal there was no water available.

The most severe form of mental torture was isolation. For this, the guards placed

The Hanoi March

In July 1966, the North Vietnamese decided to march the POWs through the streets of Hanoi to rally support for the war. The prisoners were roused from their cells, blindfolded, put into trucks, and driven to a park in Hanoi. Police officers heavily armed with rifles and bayonets lined up alongside the prisoners and marched them through the streets. The POWs who experienced the Hanoi March on July 6, 1966, will never forget it. The actions taken by the angry mob of the Vietnamese people were so extreme, the prisoners marching by the crowd feared for their lives. One Vietnamese person actually tossed a small child at the prisoners. Garbage, rocks, shoes, and all sorts of debris flew as well, and POWs were stabbed with sticks and other instruments. Captain Gerald Coffee explained the event in vivid detail in his book *Beyond Survival:*

> The shouting and chanting from both sides of the street collided right there among our ranks. It was deafening. I flashed back to the old World War II documentaries showing a million people in the Nuremberg Stadium: *Sieg Heil! Sieg Heil!* . . . The crowd grew uglier by the minute. . . . Here they were with a carte-blanche offer to focus all the pent-up frustration of their miserable war-torn lives upon those supposedly responsible. . . . Our column stalled and the hostile crowd gathered around us. The doors of the soccer stadium—of rickety metal—were kept closed by the press of the crowd.
>
> Finally the guards pried them open . . . . As in a classic soccer stadium stampede, we were swept forward in a torrent of fear and fury. . . . As the waves of faces, arms, and bodies seethed forward, children were lifted off their feet, bobbing momentarily, then disappearing with a scream. . . . Through the entry way and finally seated on the track we ministered to one another, checking the severity of gashes and bruises, and assessing the physical damages. . . . I lay back on the cinder track, closed my eyes and thought, God, what am I doing here lying in the middle of a running track bruised and bloodied by a throng of Southeast Asians. How could my life have taken such a bizarre turn?

Four American POWs are paraded through the streets of Hanoi during the Hanoi March in July 1966.

the POWs in a cell out of seeing or hearing range from other cells. This treatment might not sound brutal, but being completely alone for long periods of time can be torture. In isolation, even the strongest men could lose hope. Risner recalled the fear he faced in isolation:

The ten months I spent in a blackened cell, I went into panic. The only thing I could do was exercise, as long as I could move. It was so bad I'd put

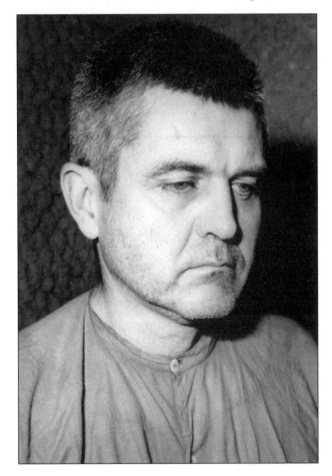

a rag in my mouth and hold another one over it so I could scream. That seemed to help. It's not that I was scared more than another time. It was happening to my mind. I had to move or die. Sometimes I'd jump up at two A.M. and exercise.[28]

Devastated by their isolation and unable to see hope in the future, a few captives committed suicide by refusing to eat.

Many senior officers who continued to exhibit control over the other prisoners were put into isolation in hopes of ending any leadership. This happened to Stockdale, who spent four and a half years not only in isolation but also in leg irons. His stamina helped him endure his torture. Stockdale said:

When I was first locked up, I was going crazy. Then I thought to myself, tough luck. You've got to get to know yourself. And you do. And after they would torture you, they would often put you in cold soak, a room where you were alone. More than anything you wanted to have another human touch. Especially so you didn't feel guilty about anything you'd said or done.[29]

Because he was a senior officer, Commander James Stockdale was kept in isolation for over four years.

How POWs Endured Torture

By the second year of captivity, a POW usually weighed about one hundred pounds. The constant malnourishment and torture left the prisoners with diminished mental abilities and emotional instability. To survive, they had to rely on their own resources. When the prisoners returned to their cells from heavy torture sessions they had to find ways to help themselves mend. They made mud casts or wood splints for their broken bones. POWs who had cell mates were luckier. Their cell mates helped snap dislocated joints back into position or bind broken bones with pieces of torn shirts. POWs alone had to find ways to lift themselves or stretch themselves to accomplish the same goals.

POWs also became resourceful at finding supplies and alternative medicines. Razors given to them before a bath were used to lance boils. To heal wounds, flies were allowed to leave their eggs, which turned into maggots that cleaned the infection. One POW who had hemorrhoids stood on his head for days. Pig fat, occasionally offered as part of a meal, was applied to chapped lips. Nibbling on charcoal scavenged from campfires helped stop diarrhea.

Lieutenant Leroy Stutz learned to survive by moving past the fear of pain. "I found out real fast how weak I was," he said. "Pain may cleanse, but it hurts. And when your shoulder rotates in your sockets and you're hanging there, you cry, and you bleed, and you pray, and you scream, and then they stuff a dirty rag in your mouth.

But the thing that affected me the most was you don't want to die here and no one even know it." [30]

Had they known from the beginning that they would be imprisoned for so long, many POWs might have given up hope. Keeping their spirits up was crucial. They had to believe they would be released any day to maintain a balance of mind and mood. "We lived by the axiom that we were never more than six months from release," remembered Lieutenant Mike Lane. "This is what kept us going." [31] Lieutenant Commander Paul Gallant agreed: "The fact that they stopped my sleep deprivation period and let me go on living was a good sign that I'd probably be going home someday. When the bombing stopped that would be a good sign. When it started again that would be a good sign. I sincerely believe that optimism is the basis of all faith and without it I'd probably have gone crazy." [32] Air force Major James Kasler said:

> Robert Louis Stevenson once said, "Anyone can carry his burden however hard until nightfall, anyone can do his work however hard for one day." This was the pattern of our lives in Hanoi during those early years of terror. We lived to endure each day hoping that nightfall would bring us a few hours of relief. We could have easily compromised our beliefs and made our lives much easier by cooperating with the Vietnamese. But our goal was to return home with our honor. Some brave men did not survive

those early years, but those who did came home with dignity and pride.[33]

In 1971, forty-five prisoners were placed together in one cell, and the men organized themselves into groups to do housekeeping chores. They also began to fill their free time by giving each other lessons, sharing their specific skills. Those who knew foreign languages taught them; a bartender explained about different wines; a former teacher taught aerodynamics and physics; a handyman instructed on home skills or auto mechanics. Major George Day said, "That was the best medicine anyone could ever receive."[34]

By sticking together—providing emotional support for each other, maintaining a military structure, and cleverly filling their time—the POWs survived some of the most brutal torture ever inflicted on American soldiers. The Vietnamese were amazed. They had been taught that the Americans were cowards. They were wrong.

Chapter 5

Resistance

The military Code of Conduct required captured soldiers to "resist by all means available," and American POWs did their best to uphold this order. This did not mean, however, that the soldiers should struggle against everything that happened in the prison camp. They were not required to fling their food back at the guards, for instance, or fight the guards barehanded when led from their cells to bathe or empty their waste bucket. "Effective resistance was not built so much on desperate goal-line stands, heroic displays of high thresholds of pain," explained Commander Stockdale. The goal instead was to send "unified, timely, persistent, committed signals to the Vietnamese that they must punish one and all, day after day, to get what they wanted." Stockdale and other senior officers realized that the POWs would accomplish more through displays of loyalty and unity than they would through individual acts of heroism. "The new guy coming in had to realize that if he was going to perform his duty . . ., he was go-

ing to make out better, he was going to get hurt less, he was going to give up less,"[35] explained Stockdale.

To help the men follow the preferred method of resistance, senior leaders informed the men what behaviors they should adopt. Stockdale coined the slogan "BACK US" to help the POWs remember what to do. Stockdale said:

Each letter had a special meaning. B—Bowing. Do not bow in public, either under camera surveillance or where nonprison observers were present. A—Air. Stay off the air. Make no broadcasts or recordings. C—Crimes. Admit to no "crimes," avoiding the use of the word in coerced confessions. K—Kiss. Do not kiss the Vietnamese goodbye, meaning show no gratitude, upon release. US—Unit over self.[36]

Unified resistance paid off immediately. Early in the war, prison camp officials

Refusing to bow to North Vietnamese officers was just one of the many forms of American resistance.

mation during interrogations. The POWs took the death threat as a bluff and refused to cooperate. The camp officials soon did away with the program and pursued other ways to obtain information. "The North Vietnamese had thought the Americans would be easy touches, and when they were not, the whole program of total subjugation was thrown into chaos," remembered Commander Denton. "There wouldn't have been much point in torturing us to death. What they wanted was to subdue us and then win us over to the point where we would routinely do their bidding. They failed."[37]

The POWs soon found that resistance could be used to focus attention on the plight of individual prisoners. Stockdale once used an organized protest to save the life of a comrade:

In 1969 [Commander] Harry Jenkins was so ill he was screaming in pain in his cell, and the guards went in and beat him instead of getting him medical attention. Some of the other POWs and I started yelling for the guards, and that got them off of him. Then I organized a fast, which lasted forty-eight hours until they finally took him out for medical care.[38]

started the "Make Your Choice" program, in which the prisoners were threatened with death if they did not reveal important infor-

Standing Together

One of the most successful resistance campaigns revolved around the freedom of the POWs to worship. Communist philosophy holds that there is no God, so the Communist guards strictly forbade any kind of worship services in the prisons. The POWs held them anyway. Every Sunday and at the same time, each man in his own cell would recite the Lord's Prayer, sing "The Star Spangled Banner," and end with the Pledge of Allegiance. The guards could torture individuals for these outbursts, but they could not torture everyone, so the services continued.

In 1970, the POWs in Camp Unity strengthened their church services. Lieutenant George Coker led the service and

Heroism Lights the Darkness

In prison, small gestures made big differences to the morale of the men who often needed the actions of another comrade to encourage them to continue resistance. Bound by his own belief in life, liberty, and the pursuit of happiness, Lieutenant Mike Christian put his convictions to the test and in the end bonded his comrades in a memory that lasted far past life in the Vietnam prison. Major Leo K. Thorness, a Medal of Honor recipient, recalled an incident that happened during 1973 at the Hanoi Hilton. A transcript of his speech is available on the P.O.W. Network website (www.pownetwork. org):

> One day as we all stood by the tank [to shower], stripped of our clothes, a young Naval pilot named Mike Christian found the remnants of a handkerchief in a gutter that ran under the prison wall. Mike managed to sneak the grimy rag into our cell and began fashioning it into a flag. Over time we all loaned him a little soap, and he spent days cleaning the material. We helped by scrounging and stealing bits and pieces of anything he could use. At night, under his mosquito net, Mike worked on the flag. He made red and blue from ground-up roof tiles and tiny amounts of ink and painted the colors onto the cloth with watery rice glue. Using thread from his own blanket and a homemade bamboo needle, he sewed on stars.

> Early in the morning a few days later, when the guards were not alert, he whispered loudly from the back of our cell, "Hey gang, look here." He proudly held up this tattered piece of cloth, waving it as if in a breeze. If you used your imagination, you could tell it was supposed to be an American flag. When he raised that smudgy fabric, we automatically stood straight and saluted, our chests puffing out, and more than a few eyes had tears. About once a week the guards would strip us, run us outside and go through our clothing. During one of those shakedowns, they found Mike's flag. . . . That night they came for him. . . . They beat him most of the night. About daylight they pushed what was left of him back through the cell door. He was badly broken, even his voice was gone. Within two weeks, despite the danger, Mike scrounged another piece of cloth and began another flag. The Stars and Stripes, our national symbol, was worth the sacrifice to him. Now, whenever I see the flag, I think of Mike and the morning he first waved that tattered emblem of a nation. It was then, thousands of miles from home in a lonely prison cell, that he showed us what it is to be truly free.

Colonel Tom Kirk led a choir. The first service was scheduled on Sunday, December 27, 1970. The men planned a combined religious and patriotic service to accommodate those who were nonbelievers. They rehearsed three songs, writing out the words on toilet paper. The next morning they began with the Pledge of Allegiance, an opening prayer, a portion of scripture recited from memory, a unison recital of the Twenty-third Psalm, a short talk by Coker, and finally the Lord's Prayer.

Toward the end of the service, the guards realized that they were watching a religious service. They gave the order that the service was not to be repeated. The next week, at the same time, another service began. Immediately, the guards appeared and ordered the men to stop talking. The POWs ignored the order. Angry, the guards removed Coker, Howard Rutledge, who had been leading the service, and Robinson Risner from the cell they shared. As they walked out, the entire group began singing "The Star Spangled Banner." When the leaders were locked into a separate cell, they could still hear the camp singing in unison.

Fearing a riot, more guards were brought in. Throughout the next week, the senior officers were pulled out for daily quizzing. Finally the guards said the men could have their services if they wrote down everything they were going to say prior to the service. Coker, Risner, and Rutledge were not allowed to return to the group, but the limited freedom to worship had been won through resistance.

Resisting Orders

The prisoners took any opportunity they could to subvert order in the prison, no matter how seemingly silly or trivial. For example, camp officials required prisoners to read propaganda aloud on radio, in front of the other inmates, or sometimes in front of the guards. Because the Vietnamese did not understand English very well, the POWs routinely mispronounced names or inserted profanity into the material to defy the authorities even as they complied with the order. In *The Passing of the Night*, Colonel Risner described how one guard began taking him out of his cell to read propaganda to him. "After a day or two of this, I discovered that he was not listening and did not know what I was reading," Risner recalled. "Sometimes I would skip a paragraph or even a page and read it any way I wanted to."[39]

Hoping they would uncover some important information about the POWs, camp commanders at the Zoo told the POWs to write about their experiences in the camp. Instead, the men wrote essays about insignificant things such as fishing or surfing. Even at the end of the war, when the mass of the prisoners were moved to a large holding cell at the Hanoi Hilton, the POWs continued to resist orders. For example, when the guards issued one razor blade to be used by seven or eight men and ordered that it be returned, the POWs refused to use the shav-

Although unified in purpose, the POWs often resisted individually. For example, Commander Denton finally agreed to make a televised confession after enduring a prolonged session of torture. When Denton entered the room and saw the lights and TV cameras, he decided to resist further. Instead of reading the statement prepared for him, Denton said the opposite. Knowing that the Vietnamese sometimes dubbed different words into the prisoner's mouth, Denton blinked his eyes in Morse code, spelling out the word "torture."

Jeremiah Denton is shown as he blinks in Morse code the word "torture" while being filmed by news cameras.

Punishment

Whether acts of resistance succeeded or failed, they usually carried a price. The guards punished resisters ruthlessly. For example, during the making of a propaganda film, the guards questioned one POW in front of the cameras, then sent him back to his cell to retrieve photos of his family. Outraged that his family would be used this way, the POW tore the photos up and sunk them in his *bo* can. He was severely beaten for this act of resistance. In another instance, Major George Day was asked if he would meet with a foreign delegation that was visiting the camps. He replied, "No. Not now. Not ever."[40] For this act of defiance, Day was beaten regularly for the next seven years. After the war was over,

ing gear. At night, the guards told the men where to sleep, but the POWs ignored these orders as well. They also refused orders to wear their shorts in the shower and instead bathed nude.

Day received the Medal of Honor for his courageous resistance.

The POWs carried their resistance into the torture chamber. They adopted the phrase "return with honor," which meant a man would not do or say anything during interrogation that he would be ashamed to tell his cell mates he had done or said. POWs adopted two forms of resistance. One was a hard line—if a guard ordered a prisoner to bow, he would remain seated until physically forced to stand even if it resulted in a beating. The other form, based on the idea that physical battles were a waste of needed energy, taught the men to let the small things go and keep their focus and energy for major battles. That idea soon became the predominant thought in all camps. POWs would still resist—maybe when ordered to bow to do it more slowly—but willing collaboration was out of the question.

Leaders of the resistance paid a high price for their actions. Senior officers such as Risner, Stockdale, and Denton were tortured regularly. Yet each time they were brutally beaten, the senior officers managed to offer no new information and continued to instruct the other men to resist. Stockdale remembered:

> Another time when the Vietnamese realized they were not getting the information they wanted in the interrogations and that everybody was withholding the same thing, they had a purge and went through the entire camp torturing everyone. My instinct told me to do something that would help my men. I broke a plate glass window and stabbed my arms with a shard of glass. Eventually, I was okay, and they asked why I did it. I said, "Because I'm not going to live like a dog anymore. I've done this for five years, and I'm not going to take it anymore." The next day the prison commissar came into the hospital room, ordered my leg irons off, and asked me to join him at a table for tea. We talked about many things, and after that day the treatment of the prisoners seemed to get better.[41]

Breaking

The officers who assumed command in the POW camps knew that the human body and mind can only stand so much torture and pain before it reaches its limit or breaking point. The breaking point was different for every man. Men who were claustrophobic would do anything before being placed in the black box in the ground. Men who were passive and could not tolerate yelling, much less brutality, might give in easier to threats of violence. As Captain Bill Baugh said, "There's a point where you've completely had it. You'll sell your mother down the river in a heartbeat. And a point that everybody reaches that decides I've had it. I've got to do something to get out of this program."[42]

For most soldiers, giving the guards what they wanted was not an option. "Even though we could sit and write something

For POWs with claustrophobia, their breaking point came when they were put into confined quarters.

for them to avoid a lot of the pain, our marching orders were different. The war was still on. They were still the enemy, and our job was either to defeat him or make his victory as difficult as possible,"[43] said Lieutenant Jerry Singleton. Some POWs decided they would rather die than help the enemy. Lieutenant Commander Bob Shumaker was one POW who made that decision. He said:

> My options were running out, and I knew I couldn't stand the pain. This had gone on for too many hours. I tried to commit suicide by banging my head against the wall and they stopped me and pulled me away. I realized I had to comply and write a confession. After I did and was put back into my cell, I cried like a baby because I felt like I had let my country down.[44]

Senior officers realized that successful resistance depended on the survival of the POWs. If all the POWs committed suicide or allowed the guards to kill them, no one would be left to resist. Eventually, the officers put out the word that when POWs reached the point during torture when they could not physically continue, they were to make up facts that seemed logical and give those to the torturers. Leaders in different camps had different ways of describing what the soldiers should do. Denton called his system the "bounce back." Denton said:

> I initiated the term bounce or roll back so that when they tortured you to the breaking point, you don't just lie back and continue to let them exploit you. You stop and give them anything. Then make them torture you again and then give them as little as you can the next time so they never advance their indoctrination of you as the object they wanted, which is for you to become a slave without torture and to do anything they want to help their cause.[45]

Escape

Escaping from a prison camp is the ultimate act of resistance, and the military Code of Conduct required POWs to attempt escapes. Because the Vietnamese prisons were dilapidated and not well maintained, escape from the compounds was not difficult. However, because of their height, skin color, and language, escaped American POWs could not blend into society outside the camps. The few who managed to escape were quickly recaptured. Some were killed for escaping.

When a prisoner escaped, every prisoner left behind in his camp was punished. So even though the Code of Conduct stipulated that POWs should try to escape, senior officers adopted a no-escape policy. "They put everyone in our camp through two weeks of hard torture," explained Baugh. "The senior officers were pulled in across the entire prison system and received hard torture. It wasn't worth it." [46]

Early Release

According to the Code of Conduct, extreme injuries or sickness and insanity were the only two reasons that a POW could be considered for an early release. Several senior officers offered lists of men who met these conditions, but the Vietnamese refused to release these prisoners. Instead they offered early release to POWs who would give them confessions. The idea of accepting early release was abhorrent to the POWs and violated the Code of Conduct. As Day put it, "Any kind of a special favor is the wrong thing regardless of how that's applied to you. An early release, better living conditions, more food, or getting something other prisoners did not get was not acceptable." [47]

The guards offered many POWs early release in exchange for signed confessions, but the Americans refused. When North Vietnamese officials learned that the father of Lieutenant Commander John McCain was a high-ranking officer, they offered the

Pictured is a model of a prison camp. Because the Vietnamese prisons were poorly maintained, escape was not difficult.

downed pilot an early release. McCain, who later served in the U.S. House and Senate, remembered the ordeal:

I was terribly wounded and broken up and in a body cast. They told me I was dying, and there would be no medical treatment unless I provided them with information. I wouldn't do that. Moments later the interrogator came into the room and asked me if my father was Admiral McCain. I said, "Yes," and they took me to the hospital where they gave me a blood transfusion, but I didn't improve. I went into a cell with Norris Overly and George Day. Day was hurt himself, so Overly washed me, fed me, and literally saved my life.

Later, when the interrogator asked if I wanted to go home, I said I'd have to think about it. Then when he came in again I said no. He said to me in English, "They taught you too well. Things are going to get worse." And they did.[48]

The rules were clear. No POW would go home until they all went home. Maintaining the proper order of release for the more than five hundred tortured and suffering prisoners remains one of the greatest accomplishments of the POWs of the Vietnam War.

Hamstrung by Congress and a public that did not fully support the war, the American military failed to accomplish its goals in Vietnam. It did not subdue the forces of North Vietnam. It did not preserve the Republic of Vietnam. Yet the military can point with pride to the courage of its soldiers, especially those held captive by the Vietnamese. Unarmed and unaided, the POWs resisted the enemy every hour of every day to the very end of the war.

Chapter 6

The POWs Go Home

Throughout their captivity, the POWs kept one thought in their minds: home. Thoughts of their release and return to their families gave prisoners a reason to live through the torture, sickness, and starvation they endured. They knew that the war would end eventually, and they wanted to be there when it did. Few could have guessed that their confinement would last not for months, but for years.

While the POWs thought of home, their loved ones at home thought of them. Unlike the POWs, their families in the United States could tell that the war in Vietnam was dragging on and the release of the POWs would not occur anytime soon. As a result, the families focused on gaining the best treatment possible for the POWs.

Afraid that any kind of attention directed toward the POWs would result in reprisals against the prisoners, the U.S. government initiated a "keep quiet" policy among the wives of POWs early in the war. Dorothy McDaniel, wife of Lieutenant Commander Eugene "Red" McDaniel, was puzzled by the telegram she received soon after her husband was shot down. She writes:

> The official telegram I had received from the Navy, the one confirming what Commander Small and the chaplain had told me, also cautioned me not to tell anyone except our immediate families that Red had been shot down over North Vietnam. "For your husband's safety and well-being," the telegram said. That was pretty persuasive language.[49]

Believing they were doing the best thing they could for their imprisoned loved ones, the POWs' wives and families, residing all over the United States and with little contact with each other, went along with the government's request for silence. Even when they heard from their loved ones in POW camps, the wives and families were left with many questions. The few letters allowed out of the POW camps were brief and gave no clue about the prisoners' welfare. Lorraine Shumaker said about her husband, Robert, "The first picture that came out he looked strong, so we knew he could withstand anything. You just lived day to day waiting for information, and we just hoped they weren't being tortured. You didn't want to believe that people could be cruel."[50]

Slowly the wives of POWs began to contact each other to exchange information and offer each other support. The more they learned, the more they began to doubt the wisdom of the "keep quiet" policy. The wives realized that in its silence, the government did not seem to be addressing the question of whether or not the prisoners were being treated according to the guidelines of the Geneva Convention.

As the war dragged on, the wives of POWs slowly began to contact one another.

POWs' Wives Take Action

After waiting for almost a year with no news of their husbands, POW wives Dorothy Mc-Daniel, Sybil Stockdale, and Louise Mulligan formed the National League of Families of American Prisoners in Southeast Asia in June 1969. Their goal was to raise the public's awareness about the POWs and soldiers missing in action (MIAs). Sybil Stockdale said:

> Never was a national organization launched more efficiently. The fact that I was already in communication with the membership and that each of us paid her own expenses simplified the organizing process. Few if any of us realized there were established procedures for formalizing an organization; we just did it the way we'd always done it when we set up a wives' club. . . .Our own simple objective was to educate the world about the Geneva Convention.[51]

The women met in groups around the country to share information and to offer moral support to each other. They wrote letters to newspaper editors, members of Congress, and foreign ambassadors, seeking help to obtain information on their loved ones. Soon they were appearing as guest speakers at functions and on local and national television programs.

The wives understood that each prisoner was an individual, not a faceless agent of the U.S. government. To help other

One Wife Takes a Stand

During the wives' campaign to bring attention to the plight of the POWs, Sybil Stockdale had targeted letters to several antiwar senators. Having once asked for a meeting with Senator Fulbright but refused, she was unwilling to give up. When she was scheduled to make an appearance on the *Today* show, she tried again. This is the letter, taken from *In Love and War*, that got her a meeting with Senator Fulbright:

January 6, 1970

Dear Senator Fulbright,

My husband is a Prisoner of War in North Vietnam and has been since September 9, 1965. Last summer, I wrote to you asking for an appointment with you and expressing the idea that the most vociferous critics of the war had probably lengthened the war and thus had a detrimental effect on the possibility of release for the Prisoners. At that time, you refused to see me on the grounds that my idea was so "preposterous" that visiting me would serve no purpose. I, and many other Americans, still believe that the critics of the war have strengthened the will of the Hanoi regime not to negotiate. I am going to be in Washington again on the 15th and 16th of January. I will be en route to the "Today" show where I have been invited to appear. When I visited with the staff at "Today" last summer, they asked me if I had talked with you and I told them you had refused to see me. I am sure they will ask me about it again. I would like to see you now to make a request that the members of our organization have asked me to see you about personally.

I hope that you may have time to visit with me on one of those two days and will wait to hear from you.

Yours Sincerely,
Mrs. James B. Stockdale

Americans see the POWs as individuals, the National League of Families began to distribute aluminum bracelets inscribed with the names of POWs and MIAs. Each band bore the name of a soldier and the date he disappeared. Millions of Americans—whether they supported the war or not—wore the silver bracelets to show their support for men they had never met and were not even sure were alive. Many sent donations to the National League of Families, which used the funds to cover administrative costs. The organization encouraged the bracelet wearers to write letters to the POWs and to wear the bracelet until the man whose name was on it came home. "We were trying to personalize it," said Phyllis Gallant, wife of Lieutenant Commander Paul Gallant. "I told the story of Paul, showed his picture, told about his life. Our goal was to have the world know what was going on so hopefully people would exert pressure on the NV to improve the treatment."[52]

Although many wives of POWs spoke out, some did not. As the war became more unpopular at home, the families of POWs sometimes were confronted by people who strongly felt that American involvement in Vietnam was immoral. Often, tempers flared as the discussions turned ugly. As a result, many families kept the identities of their loved ones secret. Henry Etta Madison, wife of Lieutenant Colonel Tom Madison, said:

It bothered me that the pilots were being called pirates and that people were so negative about the whole thing. Steve [her son] and I chose to not tell anyone that Tom was in Vietnam. I didn't want the children to tease or taunt him or for him to feel like he was different in any way because his father was a prisoner of war. So it did not bother me to be quiet about it because I wanted to protect my son.[53]

In 1969, fifty-two POW/MIA wives attended the Paris peace talks, where representatives of the United States and North Vietnam were negotiating to end the war. The wives arrived with bags filled with thousands of petitions signed by Americans. They pleaded to find out if their husbands were alive and asked for humane treatment for those in prison. North Vietnamese negotiators took tea with the women but offered nothing in the way of reassurance.

The actions of the National League of Families began to draw attention from around the world. The prime ministers of Great Britain and India, the International Red Cross, the World Council of Churches, and Pope Paul VI all issued statements asking the North Vietnamese government to follow the rules of the Geneva Convention with regards to fair treatment.

Impressed by the actions of the league, American businessman Ross Perot established an organization called United We Stand to further promote the issues of POWs and MIAs. An idea sprang up to make Christmas of 1968 special for all the POWs by flying to North Vietnam and delivering Christmas dinner to them. When insurance concerns were raised about a plane flying into a war zone, Perot agreed to buy a new plane if anything happened to the old one. Newspapers around the world carried the story about the POW relief effort, but the North Vietnamese refused to give clearance to land in Hanoi. The plane returned to the United States fully loaded. Humanitarians around the world were shocked. For the first time in the war, the government of North Vietnam suffered a major setback in the court of world opinion. As a result of the outcry, North Vietnamese government officials began to let the prisoners receive more packages from home. The North Vietnamese also began to serve the POWs a Christmas dinner. Though nothing like Christmas dinner back home, the meal did include turkey and a few vegetables. In some camps the guards began to distribute packages of treats at Christmas. Like most things in the camp, the distribution of Christmas goodies was given an odd twist by the prison officials. Before they handed the POWs the goodies, the guards first asked if the men were Protestant or Catholic. One man, who responded "neither" got nothing. Protestants received a bag containing an orange, cookies, and candy. Catholics received a tangerine instead of an orange. No one ever knew why.

Interest in the POWs grew even as the country became more divided over the war. The Junior Chamber of Commerce

As a result of worldwide public outcry, North Vietnamese officials provided the POWs with Christmas dinner.

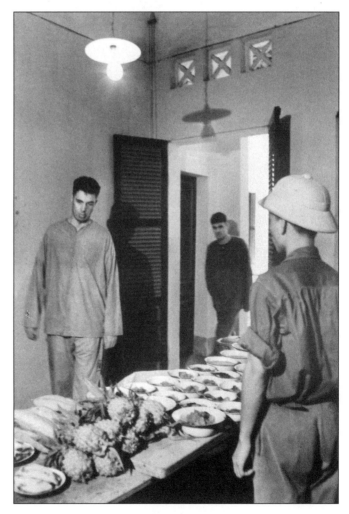

instituted the World Is Watching program aimed at focusing attention on Hanoi's treatment of the POWs. The Longshoremen's Union refused to unload Russian ships in U.S. harbors unless the Russians, who supplied the North Vietnamese government with arms and supplies, agreed to persuade Hanoi to ease up on the treatment of POWs. Many other groups across the country got on the POW bandwagon, and the White House received bags full of mail about the situation.

Under pressure from the public, the Nixon administration began to release more information about the POWs and how they were being treated. When Ho Chi Minh died on September 2, 1969, conditions improved slightly for the POWs. The North Vietnamese leaders agreed to stop treating the prisoners as war criminals. Major Guarino told the Joint Chiefs of Staff in 1973 that 70 percent of the reason conditions improved in the prisons was due to the support of the people back home. Historian John G. Hubbell agreed. "Two major factors" contributed to the improvement of POW treatment, Hubbell wrote: "the death of Ho Chi Minh; and by the time of the dictator's demise, the enormous and growing concern in the United States over the fate of those American fighting men who had fallen into Hanoi's hands."[54]

Together Again

Conditions in the battlefield also began to affect the treatment of the prisoners. In December 1970, U.S. troops raided a small prison in the countryside of Son Tay, about twenty miles from Hanoi. After an initial bombing, the Americans arrived in helicopters to liberate the POWs held in the camp. To their surprise, the prisoners had been moved a week earlier to other camps. Although the commandos failed to free any Americans, the daring raid caused the North Vietnamese to move American prisoners from the smaller camps to the Hanoi prison. More than 350 POWs were herded into an unused section of the Hanoi Hilton prison camp. It was the first time in many years the POWs were able to communicate freely with fellow Americans. "There was so much hugging and handshaking going on I had to sit down and patiently wait my turn,"[55] said Major Guarino.

The POWs called the new arrangement Camp Unity and referred to themselves as the Fourth Allied POW Wing. It was the "Fourth" because three previous wars—World Wars I, II and the Korean War—also had POWs. The term "Allied" was coined because American allies such as South Vietnamese officers and enlisted men from Thailand also were sent to the prison.

Camp Unity was located on the north side of the Hanoi prison. It formed a U shape and contained seven large, open bay cells where the men were placed forty to fifty to a cell. Major Thomas Moe later explained:

After the Son Tay raid, we were all herded to the Hanoi Hilton, but to a

Christmas Is What You Make It

For one group of prisoners who shared several Christmas seasons together, their spirit of friendship and belief sustained them. They believed it is better to give than to receive and this idea kept them busy throughout each year looking for ways to make each Christmas a little better than the last. Lieutenant Colonel Ted Ballard remembered his experiences. In his account on the P.O.W. Network website (www.pownetwork.org) he says:

> There were about thirty men in our building, three to each room. My cellmates were Captain Bob Sandvick and Captain Tom Pyle. On Christmas Eve [1967], we were taken to view a tree the Vietnamese had decorated. . . . Christmas music was played over the camp radio. [On] Christmas Day . . . the senior ranking officer of our building initiated a "Home for Christmas" prayer. Each day at noon a signal was passed to all rooms. We would then recite the Lord's Prayer.
>
> In the spring of 1968, I was moved to another camp. . . . There were twenty-nine of us in a twenty-one by twenty foot room. . . . As the [Christmas] season grew nearer the men began writing down words for holiday songs [on] toilet paper [which we] kept . . . hidden from the Vietnamese. One of the men received a package from home. He shared everything he had with the rest of us. . . . I shall never forget that Christmas Eve. A group of men quietly singing . . . "Hark, the Herald Angels Sing" and "Silent Night." Before retiring, Jim Hivner said, "Everyone who believes in Santa Claus, hang a sock on your mosquito net.". . . When I awakened the next morning I found a Christmas card inside my net. The other men had one in their stockings. . . .
>
> [Christmas of 1969] we made Christmas cards for the men in the other buildings. These were "air-mailed" by tying a rock to the paper and throwing them from our courtyard to theirs. For a Christmas tree, we decorated a small Swiss-type broom with strips of cloth and paper with various designs. Mike McGrath was quite a good artist. . . . He used one of his black pajama tops as a background and drew a tree on it. From paper and cloth he made stars and ornaments and attached them to the tree. Small packages with each of our names were also attached. This was kept hidden during the day but was hung on the wall in the evenings for our enjoyment. We exchanged gifts, both real and imaginary. Before retiring we each tied a stocking to our nets. Early Christmas morning . . . our stockings were full of candy, gifts, and greeting cards.
>
> [Christmas of 1970] was a fairly good one for us. . . . Christmas Eve the men put on an outstanding play. It was the POW version of Charles Dickens' "Christmas Carol." [On] Christmas morning . . . Tom McNish . . . was running up and down the long room with a large bag slung over his shoulder. . . . Then he set down his bag, opened it, and out jumped Santa. Rod Knutson had on a red suit, black "boots," stocking cap, and a white beard. I never found out where or how they scrounged all that material.
>
> [Christmas of 1971] Dwight Sullivan presented me with a small poker table which he made from bread and sticks. I gave my friend Leroy Stutz an imaginary book, "How to Play Winning Poker.". . .
>
> Christmas Eve, 1972, was a quiet one. The choir sang some carols and that was about it. Our thoughts and prayers were about the future.

section we had never seen before. The rooms were very large and held about 50 people each. They put 60 to 70 of us in these rooms. We slept on concrete slabs and were packed so tightly that we had to sleep on our sides; there was not enough room to lay on our backs or stomachs. We had one person's head in front of our face, and one person's head behind our head. To roll over, you had to raise yourself up and sort of flip over to the other side. I still tend to roll over in bed this way.[56]

Treatment of the POWs noticeably improved. The North Vietnamese continued to punish prisoners for breaking the rules, but the daily torture sessions came to an end. The delivery of packages from home became more frequent, and items such as decks of cards and long johns were passed on to the prisoners.

When U.S. forces began to raid smaller prison camps, the North Vietnamese closed them. POWs at the Hanoi Hilton were herded together into larger cells to make room for prisoners brought from the smaller camps.

A Message from the Sky

For years, the North Vietnamese and the Americans had been close to signing a peace agreement, but time after time the deal fell through. Frustrated with the latest collapse, President Nixon tried to force the North Vietnamese back to the bargaining table by resuming the bombing of North Vietnam, which the United States had halted four years earlier as a condition for starting the peace talks. On December 18, 1972, Nixon unleashed the most intense bombing raids since the end of World War II. The POWs held in and around Hanoi rejoiced at the sound of the attack. Major Samuel Johnson writes:

I was half-asleep, cold and uncomfortable under my thin blankets, when I heard sounds in the distance. *That's not thunder.* . . . I was suddenly wide awake. *Aircraft! B-52s!* The next night around midnight, explosions again erupted in the silence. . . .Instinctively, everyone in the room dropped to the floor. . . . The sky was filled with dozens of B-52s, each carrying a capacity load of more than a hundred bombs. The sounds of the bombs hurtling through the air sounded like hordes of geese in flight. As they hit the ground and began to explode one by one across the city, we covered our ears and dove against the walls in search of some kind of shelter. The roar was unrelenting. It was as if every gun and every missile in the city were firing simultaneously with the explosion of the American bombs.[57]

Prison guards, concerned about their own safety, retreated to the hills for shelter. The day after the bombing had temporarily ceased, guards returned, bringing the prisoners extra beds made of wood to use as shelter in case the bombing resumed. It did. For the next eleven nights, American aircraft pounded North Vietnam in what became known as the Christmas Bombing. The raids ended on December 29, 1972. The next day, the North Vietnamese agreed to negotiate further. On January 23, 1973, President Nixon addressed the nation to announce an end to the war and the fate of the POWs:

Good evening. I have asked for this radio and television time tonight for the purpose of announcing that we today have concluded an agreement to end the war and bring peace with honor in Vietnam and in Southeast Asia. The following statement is being issued at this moment in Washington and Hanoi:

At 12:30 Paris time today [Tuesday], January 23, 1973, the Agreement on Ending the War and Restoring Peace in Vietnam was initialed by Dr. Henry Kissinger on behalf of the United States, and Special Adviser Le Duc Tho on behalf of the Democratic

Republic of Vietnam. The agreement will be formally signed by the parties participating in the Paris Conference on Vietnam on January 27, 1973, at the International Conference Center in Paris. The cease-fire will take effect at 2400 Greenwich Mean Time, January 27, 1973. The United States and the Democratic Republic of Vietnam express the hope that this agreement will insure stable peace in Vietnam and contribute to the preservation of lasting peace in Indochina and Southeast Asia.

That concludes the formal statement. . . .

A cease-fire, internationally supervised, will begin at 7 p.m., this Saturday, January 27, Washington time. Within 60 days from this Saturday, all Americans held prisoners of war throughout Indochina will be released. There will be

On January 23, 1973, President Nixon informed the nation about the end of the Vietnam War and the fate of the POWs.

the fullest possible accounting for all of those who are missing in action.[58]

At the Hanoi Hilton, Dog, one of the most feared guards, assembled the prisoners to inform them of their fate. He told the POWs that they would be leaving North Vietnam in groups of 150 men every two weeks. The sick and wounded were to be released first. The remaining prisoners would be released in order of capture. After Dog dismissed the prisoners, Colonel Risner did an about-face and called the Fourth Allied POW Wing to attention. The 400 men snapped to attention, the squadron commanders saluted, eight hundred pairs of tire-tread sandals slapped together, and in unison each commander ordered his units dismissed. As prisoners moved into their cells, some shouted with glee, exchanging slaps and hugs with their comrades. Others shuffled back to their cells quietly. The emotion was too much. They could not believe they were really going home.

The End at Last

Prisoners from South Vietnam and Laos, including several civilian prisoners and two women—one a missionary and the other a German nurse—were brought to the Hanoi prison to leave with the other prisoners. On February 11, 1973, the night before the release program began, the POWs were given showers, haircuts, new clothes, shoes, and two duffel bags. Some prisoners took souvenirs of their captivity—their old pajamas or their tin cup. Other POWs bore only the scars on their bodies and in their memories.

Some POWs had imagined that the day of their release would be boisterous and happy. Instead the prisoners walked out of their camps without a sound. Lieutenant Junior Grade Everett Alvarez Jr. described the subdued atmosphere:

A lot of us old timers really were emotionally drained and thought, "I'll believe it when I see it." I was so emotionally drained from despair and failures in the past, the close friends I'd lost, and the people we lived with that we never saw again. You became cold and developed a shroud of protection so that you wouldn't let your emotions run away. The emotional shield that develops is a protectiveness to be able to cope, and it took a long time to break that shield so that you became a warm person again. It was hard to show emotion to the point where you shed tears.[59]

The Vietnamese prison officials told the first group that left the prison to walk out with their heads bowed. Instead, the American soldiers marched in step with their heads held high, making a precise column-right maneuver at the bus door. The bus drove through Hanoi to the airport where the troops filed in formation to cross the debarkation line. The soldiers were required to shake hands with the North Vietnamese officials before stepping across the line. Next they shook hands with American officials. Then they

Homeward Bound

Aboard the bus and heading away from prison—the home some POWs had known for more than ten years—the men began to believe maybe this was really it. According to *Honor Bound: The History of American Prisoners of War in Southeast Asia, 1961–1973* by Stuart Rochester and Frederick Kiley,

> As the convoy wove its way through the downtown traffic to the airport, Coffee "felt a little weird, like a tourist on a tour bus." Denton remembered their being "subdued in the solemnity of our thoughts, almost hypnotized. . . ." During a stop at an administration building on the outskirts of Gia Lam, the prisoners were offered sandwiches and beer before reboarding the buses, arriving at the terminal around noon just as the first of three U.S. Air Force C-141s was landing. The spectacle of the giant transport touching down was "electrifying," Alvarez recalled. "It was the first C-141 I had ever seen, and it was love at first sight." Guarino remembered being detached until the cargo door opened and "people started jumping down from the airplane, people I had forgotten existed, who looked to me like they were from another world. *Yes,* they were from another world . . . *our* world."

A group of released prisoners shakes hands with U.S. officials as they board a plane for home.

boarded the plane. The first moment of happiness came when female nurses on board the aircraft hugged them. Each man was given a cup of coffee and a doughnut. All personnel were quiet as the wheels of the plane lifted off the ground. Once in the air, the pilot announced that they had just left Vietnam and congratulated the men.

Pandemonium broke out. As one soldier described it, the men had gone "from the depths of the dark ages to sweetness and light in forty-five minutes." [60]

Am I Really Free?

The soldiers were taken to Clark Air Force Base in the Philippines for formal debriefings—days where they were examined and questioned to learn details of their imprisonment. They moved through halls covered with Valentine's Day decorations home made by the children attending the base school to welcome the POWs back. For the first time in years, the soldiers received checkups and dental care. The POWs remained at the base for a few days so they could adjust to their sudden freedom. Immediately the soldiers noticed the small things they once would have taken for granted. "The soft music that played in the background at the hospital, the pretty nurses, the soft beds, and the soft sheets, were amazing," [61] recalled Captain George McKnight.

For some of the men the soft beds were almost impossible to sleep on after sleeping on boards for many years. Many of them had calluses on their tailbones, hips, knees, elbows, and ankles from sleeping on concrete. The nurses treated them to massages.

The Red Cross rigged a telephone line to the United States, and every man got to phone home.

The canteen on the base where the men ate became a hangout, and the men were allowed to order whatever they wanted to eat. One man ordered a steak and twelve eggs over easy, then returned thirty minutes later for another dozen eggs. Although they all had big eyes for what they imagined they wanted to eat, some found it difficult to finish an entire meal. Their stomachs had shrunk so much, they could only manage small nibbles at a time. Lieutenant Ron Bliss said, "For me it was the ice. They had big pitchers of water with real ice in our rooms. That's how I knew I was home." [62]

For Colonel Risner, realization came the next day. "As I was putting on my uniform jacket, I looked down at those buttons [with the stars and eagle] and I had to cry. That was my release." [63]

Lieutenant Commander John McCain said, "I didn't care about food. I wanted to read and know all the things that had happened while we were away." [64]

Lieutenant Ed Mechenbier realized his and the other POWs' fortune at coming home. "I thought, *we were lucky*. Some of the men will never have this opportunity. How many guys did we leave behind who never got the chance to be a prisoner? It beats the heck out of being killed. We weren't heroes—just unlucky guys who got to serve in very different circumstances. Others didn't—the people who never got to come home."[65]

Each returning soldier was assigned a junior escort officer to help him reestablish his life. The escort officers answered questions, scheduled appointments and meetings, and took care of details such as making sure the soldier received all his back pay.

Fears and Misgivings

Many former POWs had mixed feelings about seeing their families. While eager to embrace their loved ones, the returning soldiers also feared misunderstanding and rejection. Some worried that their drastic weight loss, aging, and scars might upset or even repulse their wives, fiancées, and other loved ones. Some feared that their spouses and family members would lose respect for them if they knew all the things they had done to survive. They also wondered if they would fit into a world full of comforts and pleasures after such a prolonged period of deprivation and brutality. Before his release, Lieutenant Commander Hugh Al Stafford weighed his own mixed feelings as he wrote a note to himself on a cigarette paper:

Release could be a dangerous and traumatic period. People are not as sympathetic as you expect. Loved ones may be dead or no longer love you. You were acutely alive to yourself all those years, but partly dead to them. . . . You may resent changes in them that you would not have detected had you been there to change with them. Your years of trial and soul-searching emotional agony in prison may not end with mere release. The first days and weeks of rehabilitation can be fraught with danger, too. Have faith. Once the trial is over, all of it . . . the years in prison and disillusionments of return, you will be able to regard it as one big nightmare and then press on with life. Carry with you that nothing will be that bad again.[66]

The families of the former POWs also looked forward to the reunion with a mixture of joy and dread. Some wives worried that the long separation might have changed the relationship they had with their husbands. "I hadn't seen my husband for six years and was worried,"[67] recalled Henry Etta Madison, wife of Major Tom Madison.

Some children of former POWs had either never met their fathers or had been too young to remember them. For these children, the reunion actually would be a first meeting. "I was concerned about our son Grant," recalled Lorraine Shumaker, wife of Lieutenant Commander Robert Shumaker. "He was shy and I wondered how he would react. I asked him, 'what are you going to do when Dad comes off the plane?' and he shrugged. I said, 'I'm going to run up and give him a big kiss and I'll beat you.'"[68]

Families Reunited

For many families, the doubts and fears disappeared when the former POWs reached home. In a letter home, Lieutenant Commander Robert Shumaker had asked his wife to wear a miniskirt to the airport when he arrived. "The mini skirt had already gone out of style, but I wore one," Lorraine Shumaker recalled. Grant Shumaker did not hesitate to embrace his father. "I said, 'there's your dad,'" Lorraine Shumaker remembered. "Grant ran up to Bob and he grabbed him up in his arms and then I ran out to greet him."[69] Henry Etta Madison

---

"We're Home"

Upon arrival at Travis Air Force Base where many of the POWs who lived in the western states would take flights home, Commander Stockdale was asked to make a speech, taken from *In Love and War,* which was repeated by Eric Sevareid that night on the national news. Stockdale said:

> For the past seven or eight years, I doubt that there was a prisoner of war in Hanoi who did not occasionally hum that old refrain, "California Here We Come." Well, California, we have come. I'm proud to be the representative of this group of wonderful warriors right behind me, and to express to you people here our heartfelt thanks for your loyalty to us. The men who followed me down that ramp know what loyalty means, because they have been living with loyalty, living off loyalty for the past several years. I mean loyalty to our military ethic, loyalty to our commander in chief, loyalty to each other. And now we're home to rest and regain our strength to continue productive lives. As that Athenian warrior and poet Sophocles wrote over 2400 years ago, "Nothing is so sweet as to return home from sea and listen to the raindrops of home." We're home. America, America, God shed His grace on thee.

A returning POW is greeted by his family as he arrives at Travis Air Force Base in California.

remembered that her concerns melted away as soon as she and her husband "actually spoke."[70]

The former POWs expressed a wide range of emotions. Some felt a surge of patriotism. Commander Denton stepped from the plane and gave a short speech. Barely able to control his emotions, he said, "We are honored we've had the opportunity to serve our country under difficult circumstances. We are profoundly grateful to our Commander in Chief and to our nation for this day. God Bless America."[71]

Captain Laird Guttersen, who received four purple hearts for combat in Vietnam, could not forget his fallen comrades. Upon his return to the United States, he said, "I am a saddened man, amidst the wonderment and joy of homecoming, for so many of my comrades-in-arms cannot share in this joy. For them I am a determined man. I shall never turn my back on the true heroes of this war—those who died and those, if any, still MIA."[72]

As families reunited, the former POWs learned of many things their loved ones did to pass time until they came home. Sometimes, even the simplest things were the most amazing. Shirley Johnson, the wife of Colonel Samuel Johnson, told her husband that she sometimes sat on the front steps of their Texas home at night and stared at the stars because she knew he was not able to. It was the only thing she could think of to do for him. Hearing the story, Colonel Johnson wept.

Similar scenes were repeated throughout the nation. After as many as eight years and countless other silent vigils, the POWs were home.

The Legacy of Vietnam POWs

The return of the POWs sparked a burst of patriotism from the American public. From the moment President Nixon announced that the war was over and the POWs would be coming home, the families of POWs began to receive good wishes from friends and strangers alike. Flowers, bottles of champagne, and mail arrived at every POW's house. The national television networks broadcast the first reunions of the former POWs and their families. Practically every POW's hometown welcomed him or her home with fanfare—banners, parades, and monuments. Some even had streets renamed in their honor. In May 1973 the White House had a dinner honoring all the POWs. Many celebrities and military officials attended.

Army Specialist 6 John Sparks, who spent six years in captivity, was moved by the welcome:

I've learned much about myself and my country, enough to really know what my country and its people mean to me.

There could have been no greater show of people's love for their country than the welcome they gave us upon our return, and I will forever be grateful to them for it, for giving me a new life, a life without cause to suffer or to look, with great expectation, toward a more meaningful future.[73]

Silence and Scorn

The celebration was brief. The nation had been deeply divided on Vietnam for many years with millions of Americans believing the war was not merely bad policy, but illegal and even immoral. When the public learned about the massacre of about five hundred Vietnamese civilians—including women and children—by American troops in the village of My Lai, millions were outraged at the conduct of American forces. When the public learned that the Nixon administration, which had maintained that it would not expand the war to nations that border Vietnam, had secretly bombed Viet Cong forces in Cambodia, more outrage followed. Many Americans became angry about having been lied to by their leaders. Protests against the war became a daily occurrence across the country. In 1970, a protest at Kent State University ended with National Guard troops firing their weapons at the protesters and killing four students. The war provoked heated discussions in the media, classrooms, churches, and family dinner tables across the country. The wounds were deep, and the end of the war did not heal them.

The former POWs and other veterans were often accosted in airports or on the street. Sometimes they were spat on or called "baby killers" because they had bombed villages in Vietnam where innocent people lived. These incidents were especially hard for the former POWs to understand, because they had not heard details about the antiwar movement while they were in prison and the protests had ended long before they returned to the United States. Other soldiers returning from wars had been honored and respected. The Vietnam veterans were ignored or scorned.

Some former POWs faced other difficulties as well. Some experienced flashbacks in which they relived scenes of their captivity. Others flinched or became tense at the sound of firecrackers, automobile backfires, and other sudden sounds. Some-

times they had nightmares about their treatment and would jump up during their sleep or flail about in bed. Some experienced outbursts of anger, lack of concentration, and emotional dysfunction. Soldiers in other wars had exhibited similar behavior, which was called "shell shock" in World War I and "battle fatigue" in World War II. After the Vietnam War, psychologists named the condition post–traumatic stress disorder, or PTSD, and began to develop treatments for it.

According to a long-term study organized by Captain Robert Mitchell, a naval flight surgeon, as a group the former POWs emerged from the war in better shape than their comrades in the field. There were no long-term psychiatric cases among the POWs, none were committed to mental facilities, and only one committed suicide. Mitchell believed the outcome was due to the POWs' spirit of teamwork and resistance. He said, "They were well-trained, well-motivated men who believed in something. A similar group taken at random, probably wouldn't have done nearly so well."[74]

Surprisingly, the POWs proved to be in better physical health than other veterans, too. The former POWs received annual checkups that included a battery of tests. At the same time each man was assigned a counterpart, a man close to his physical characteristics that had not been a POW and who was also monitored every year. Fifteen years after the program started it was determined that the POWs had better health than those who had not been pris-

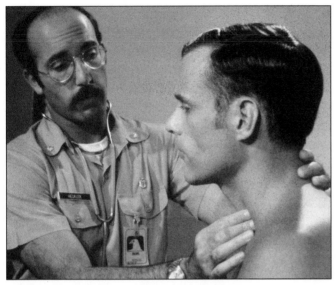

Annual checkups revealed that POWs had better health than those who had not been prisoners.

oners. Untreated lingering injuries not included, the overall general health and the POWs' cardiovascular conditions resulted in fewer heart attacks than in the other group of men.

Telling the Story

Because conditions in the prison camps had been kept secret from the world, the former POWs found that few Americans had any idea of what they had been through. Some former POWs began to speak out about their experience. In 1973, Colonel Robinson Risner published his firsthand account of the POW camps, *The Passing of the Night*. Books by other POWs and veterans followed. In 1979, Vietnam veteran Tim

O'Brien received the National Book Award for his novel, *Going After Cacciato*, a surrealistic account of the actions of a private serving in Vietnam. More than one hundred movies touched on the Vietnam experience, further acquainting Americans with details about the war. Vietnam veteran Oliver Stone wrote and directed the 1986 motion picture *Platoon*, which received eight Academy Award nominations and received four awards, including best picture and best director.

The most powerful monument to the Vietnam War arose from one Vietnam veteran's personal anguish. In 1979, Jan Scruggs had one of many nightmares about the war. The next morning, he vowed to build a memorial that would be inscribed with the name of every American who had died in the war. It took years to raise the money required to build the memorial, but Scruggs persevered. The sponsors of the memorial held a competition to find a suitable plan for the monument. Maya Ying Lin, a twenty-one-year-old architecture student, submitted the winning design. Lin's plans called for the construction of a V shaped, tapered wall of black granite that would rise from the grassy site in Washington, D.C., then gradually sink back into it. The names of the 58,132 Americans who died in the war or were missing in action were to be carved into the polished face of the stone.

Dedicated on Memorial Day 1982, the Vietnam Veterans Memorial has become the most visited monument in Washington, D.C. Each day, hundreds of people visit the solemn site known simply as "The Wall." Many people leave behind objects of personal meaning. Vietnam veterans have left behind medals won in combat. Family and friends leave letters, notes, cards, jewelry, photo albums, even baked goods such as pies. Those who supported the war and those who opposed it are equally moved by the memorial. James Quay, executive director of the California Council for Humanities, who was a conscientious objector during the Vietnam War, described his visit to the Wall:

I found the name of a man who had been killed just as I had publicly begun to oppose the war. What would we have said to one another if we'd met then in July of 1967? What would we say to one another now? Touching the names only makes us feel how far away they are. They must remain there, united by their shared catastrophe, while we, the living, must leave, united by our shared grief.... Important differences between us may remain, but the Memorial has given us something still more important—the common ground of grief. So long as grief is heartfelt, shared, and remembered—always—there is hope for peace, and so for us all.[75]

As divisions over the war healed, Americans began to realize that the general lack of support for the Vietnam veterans had been damaging to many of them. The next time the United States fought a war, things were different. Support for U.S. troops in the Persian Gulf War was overwhelming. People marched in the streets, wore T-shirts and hats printed with slogans of support, and sent thousands of packages to soldiers they did not even know.

The former POWs remain proud of the service they gave to their country. Lieutenant Colonel Arthur Ballard said in reflection, "I wish every American could have witnessed the individual courage, the devotion to duty, and the unswerving patriotism of our fighting men during our years of captivity."[76] The former POWs are also proud of the contributions they were able to make to the armed services after the war. As prisoners, they learned the importance of adjusting prior military rules about resistance. Previous military codes subscribed to a system that offered soldiers no leeway during torture. The bounce back policy initiated in Vietnam kept many POWs alive. It became the logical, inevitable standard that relieved a man from the guilt of giving in and enabled him to adhere to the "keep faith with your fellow prisoner" policy. After the war, the armed forces incorporated the lessons of bounce back into their doctrine and began to teach it in their survival schools.

For some POWs, the healing that took place in the United States did not end the conflicts they felt about the war. A few felt they had left unfinished busi-

Hundreds of people visit the Vietnam Veterans Memorial each day to honor the Americans who served in Vietnam.

ness in Vietnam. Since 1972 many former POWs, alone or in groups, have returned to the country of their imprisonment. Some have visited South Vietnamese citizens they made friends with during the war. Others have toured the prisons where they were held. A few realized that the war would not be over for them until they had forgiven their captors and even their torturers. As Commander Howard Rutledge, a prisoner for seven and a half years, put it, "I'm sure the enemy had families who bled and died. I'm sure the enemy cried when loved ones went away and did not return. I'm sure the enemy, too, were tempted to give way to anger and hatred. But revenge is God's business. When it's over, we must try to forget and forgive." [77]

☆ Notes ☆

Introduction: The Longest War in American History

1. Sam Johnson and Jan Winebrenner, *Captive Warriors*. College Station: Texas A&M University Press, 1992, p. 10.
2. Quoted in the film *Return with Honor*, produced and directed by Freida Lee Mock and Terry Sanders. Santa Monica, CA: American Film Foundation, 1999.
3. James Stockdale, interview by author, October 4, 1999.

Chapter 1: Face to Face with the Enemy

4. Quoted in the film *Return with Honor*.
5. Gerald Coffee, *Beyond Survival: Building on the Hard Times—a POW's Inspiring Story*. New York: G. P. Putnam's Sons, 1990, p. 24.
6. Coffee, *Beyond Survival*, p. 24.
7. Quoted in the film *Return with Honor*.
8. Quoted in P.O.W. Network, "Biographies of Prisoners of War and Missing in Action from the Vietnam Conflict," www.pownetwork.org.

Chapter 2: Home Not-So-Sweet Home

9. Quoted in Stuart I. Rochester and Frederick Kiley, *Honor Bound: The History of American Prisoners of War in Southeast Asia, 1961–1973*. Annapolis, MD: Naval Institute Press, 1998, p. 424.
10. Quoted in P.O.W. Network, "Biographies of Prisoners of War and Missing in Action."
11. Quoted in Larry Guarino, *A POW's Story: 2801 Days in Hanoi*. New York: Ballantine Books, 1990, p. 33.
12. Quoted in P.O.W. Network, "Biographies of Prisoners of War and Missing in Action."
13. Quoted in Rochester and Kiley, *Honor Bound*, p. 124.

Chapter 3: Communication: A Key to Survival and Resistance

14. Stockdale, interview.
15. John McCain and Mark Salter, *Faith of My Fathers*. New York: Random House, 1999, p. 214.

Chapter 4: Torture and Isolation

16. Quoted in P.O.W. Network, "Biographies of Prisoners of War and Missing in Action."
17. Johnson and Winebrenner, *Captive Warriors*, p. 180.
18. Quoted in P.O.W. Network, "Biographies of Prisoners of War and Missing in Action."

19. Quoted in P.O.W. Network, "Biographies of Prisoners of War and Missing in Action."

20. Quoted in the film *Return with Honor*.

21. Robinson Risner, *The Passing of the Night: My Seven Years as a Prisoner of the North Vietnamese*. New York: Random House, 1973, p. 158.

22. Risner, *The Passing of the Night*, p. 82.

23. Johnson and Winebrenner, *Captive Warriors*, p. 47.

24. Johnson and Winebrenner, *Captive Warriors*, p. 169.

25. Quoted in the film *Return with Honor*.

26. Quoted in the film *Return with Honor*.

27. Risner, *The Passing of the Night*, p. 80.

28. Quoted in the film *Return with Honor*.

29. Stockdale, interview.

30. Quoted in the film *Return with Honor*.

31. Mike Lane, interview by author, October 21, 1999.

32. Quoted in P.O.W. Network, "Biographies of Prisoners of War and Missing in Action."

33. Quoted in P.O.W. Network, "Biographies of Prisoners of War and Missing in Action."

34. Quoted in P.O.W. Network, "Biographies of Prisoners of War and Missing in Action."

Chapter 5: Resistance

35. James Stockdale and Sybil Stockdale, *In Love and War: The Story of a Family's Ordeal and Sacrifice During the Vietnam Years*. Annapolis, MD: Naval Institute Press, 1990, p. 247.

36. Quoted in John Morrocco and the Editors of the Boston Publishing Company, *Thunder from Above: Air War, 1941–1968*. Boston: Boston Publishing, 1984, p. 76.

37. Quoted in Rochester and Kiley, *Honor Bound*, p. 226.

38. Stockdale, interview.

39. Risner, *The Passing of the Night*, p. 155.

40. Quoted in Johnson and Winebrenner, *Captive Warriors*, p. 82.

41. Stockdale, interview.

42. Quoted in the film *Return with Honor*.

43. Quoted in P.O.W. Network, "Biographies of Prisoners of War and Missing in Action."

44. Quoted in the film *Return with Honor*.

45. Quoted in the film *Return with Honor*.

46. Quoted in the film *Return with Honor*.

47. Quoted in the film *Return with Honor*.

48. Quoted in the film *Return with Honor*.

Chapter 6: The POWs Go Home

49. Dorothy McDaniel, *After the Hero's Welcome: A POW Wife's Story of the Battle Against a New Enemy*. Chicago: Bonus Books, 1991, p. 39.

50. Quoted in the film *Return with Honor*.

51. Stockdale and Stockdale, *In Love and War*, p. 313.

52. Quoted in the film *Return with Honor*.

53. Quoted in the film *Return with Honor*.

54. John G. Hubbell, *P.O.W.: A Definitive History of the American Prisoner-of-War Experience in Vietnam, 1964–1973*. New York: Reader's Digest Press, 1976, p. 519.

55. Quoted in Rochester and Kiley, *Honor Bound*, p. 523.
56. Thomas Moe, interview by author, October 22, 1999.
57. Johnson and Winebrenner, *Captive Warriors*, p. 268.
58. Richard Nixon, broadcast address, January 23, 1973, available at www.metalab.unc.edu/pub/academic/history/marshall/military/vietnam/policies.and.politics/paris_peace_1973.txt.
59. Quoted in the film *Return with Honor.*
60. Quoted in the film *Return with Honor.*
61. Quoted in the film *Return with Honor.*
62. Quoted in the film *Return with Honor.*
63. Quoted in the film *Return with Honor.*
64. Quoted in the film *Return with Honor.*
65. Quoted in P.O.W. Network, "Biographies of Prisoners of War and Missing in Action."
66. Quoted in Geoffrey Norman, *Bouncing Back: How a Heroic Band of POWs Survived Vietnam.* Boston: Houghton Mifflin, 1990, p. 214.
67. Quoted in the film *Return with Honor.*
68. Quoted in the film *Return with Honor.*
69. Quoted in the film *Return with Honor.*
70. Quoted in the film *Return with Honor.*
71. Quoted in the film *Return with Honor.*
72. Quoted in P.O.W. Network, "Biographies of Prisoners of War and Missing in Action."

Epilogue: The Legacy of the Vietnam POWs

73. Quoted in P.O.W. Network, "Biographies of Prisoners of War and Missing in Action."
74. Quoted in Norman, *Bouncing Back*, p. 244.
75. Quoted in *The American Experience in Vietnam.* Norman: University of Oklahoma, 1989, p. 301.
76. Quoted in P.O.W. Network, "Biographies of Prisoners of War and Missing in Action."
77. Quoted in the film *Return with Honor.*

★ For Further Reading ★

Patience H. C. Mason, *Recovering from the War.* New York: Viking, 1990. This is a women-focused guide to helping vets, families, and oneself deal with the problems of returning soldiers from the Vietnam War.

George J. Veith, *Code—Name Bright Light:* *The Untold Story of U.S. POW Rescue During the Vietnam War.* Free Press, 1998. Reports from the author who polled former military personnel involved in efforts to liberate POWs. A genuine contribution to a historical understanding of the Vietnam conflict.

✫ Works Consulted ✫

Books

The American Experience in Vietnam. Norman: University of Oklahoma, 1989. Provides an in-depth analysis that clarifies the historical phenomena of the Vietnam era from various perspectives.

Peter Arnett, *Live from the Battlefield.* New York: Simon and Schuster, 1994. Accounts with photos of Peter Arnett's thirty-five years of news coverage in war zones.

Gerald Coffee, *Beyond Survival: Building on the Hard Times—a POW's Inspiring Story.* New York: G. P. Putnam's Sons, 1990. A navy pilot's inspiring story of survival during imprisonment in a POW camp.

Clark Dougan, Samuel Lipsman, and the Editors of the Boston Publishing Company. *The Vietnam Experience.* Boston: Boston Publishing, 1984. Provides in-depth analyses that clarify the historical phenomena of the Vietnam era from various perspectives.

Larry Guarino, *A POW's Story: 2801 Days in Hanoi.* New York: Ballantine Books, 1990. The personal experience of Guarino during his imprisonment in a POW camp.

Zalin Grant, *Survivors.* New York: Da Capo Press, 1994. A straightforward account by nine Vietnam War POWs of their experiences as prisoners.

George C. Herring, *America's Longest War.* 2nd ed., New York: Newberry Awards Records, 1979. Historical accounts of the Vietnam War.

John G. Hubbell, *P.O.W.: A Definitive History of the American Prisoner-of-War Experience in Vietnam, 1964–1973.* New York: Reader's Digest Press, 1976. .

Monica Jensen-Stevenson and William Stevenson, *Kiss the Boys Goodbye.* New York: Penguin Books, 1990. Accounts of two journalists who believe the American government withheld important information in matters relating to the POWs of the Vietnam War.

Sam Johnson and Jan Winebrenner, *Captive Warriors.* College Station: Texas A&M University Press, 1992. Sam Johnson's personal account of his experiences as a POW in the Vietnam War.

John McCain and Mark Salter, *Faith of My Fathers.* New York: Random House, 1999. Discusses the careers of three generations of McCains including some of John McCain's years as a POW in the Vietnam War.

Dorothy McDaniel, *After the Hero's Welcome: A POW Wife's Story of the Battle Against a New Enemy.* Chicago: Bonus Books, 1991. A POW wife's story of the battle against a new enemy—the fight against American politics.

John Morrocco and the Editors of the Boston Publishing Company, *Thunder from Above: Air War, 1941–1968*. Boston: Boston Publishing, 1984. An overall view of the Vietnam War with a heavy emphasis on the mechanics and statistics of the war.

Geoffrey Norman, *Bouncing Back: How a Heroic Band of POWs Survived Vietnam*. Boston: Houghton Mifflin, 1990. Hugh Al Stafford's story of his years as a Vietnam POW.

Robinson Risner, *The Passing of the Night: My Seven Years as a Prisoner of the North Vietnamese*. New York: Random House, 1973. Robinson Risner's personal account of his experiences as a POW in the Vietnam War.

Stuart I. Rochester and Frederick Kiley, *Honor Bound: The History of American Prisoners of War in Southeast Asia, 1961–1973*. Annapolis, MD: Naval Institute Press, 1998. Detailed documented experiences of Vietnam POWs.

James Stockdale, *A Vietnam Experience*. Stanford, CA: Hoover Press, 1984. Ten years of personal reflection by Stockdale about the Vietnam War. Includes many of his speeches made since returning home from the war.

James Stockdale and Sybil Stockdale, *In Love and War: The Story of a Family's Ordeal and Sacrifice During the Vietnam Years*. Annapolis, MD: Naval Institute Press, 1990. Accounts by the Stockdales of their lives during and after the Vietnam War.

Truong Nhu Tang, David Chanoff, and Doan Van Toai, *A Viet Cong Memoir*. New York: Random House, 1986. The life story of revolutionary Truong Nhu Tang and his accounts of the political upheavals of Vietnam.

Periodicals
Time, April 9, 1971.

Interviews
James Stockdale, interview by author, October 4, 1999.

Mike Lane, interview by author, October 21, 1999.

Thomas Moe, interview by author, October 22, 1999.

Films
Return with Honor, produced and directed by Frieda Lee Mock and Terry Sanders. Santa Monica, CA: American Film Foundation, 1999. An emotional and true story of the American pilots shot down over Vietnam that explores their heroism, faith, endurance, and brotherhood.

Internet Sources
Richard Nixon, broadcast address, January 23, 1973. Available at www.metalab.unc. edu/pub/academic/history/marshall/ military/vietnam/policies.and.politics/ paris_peace_1973.txt.

P.O.W. Network, "Biographies of Prisoners of War and Missing in Action from the Vietnam Conflict." Available at www. pownetwork.org.

☆ Index ☆

★ Picture Credits ★

★ About the Authors ★

Diana Saenger is a journalist and newspaper editor who specializes in the entertainment field. The author of *Everyone Wants My Job: The ABCs of Entertainment Writing*, published by Piccadilly Press, she is a syndicated film critic and past president of the San Diego Film Critic's Society. She has an AS degree from Grossmont College in El Cajon, California.

Ms. Saenger has one son, two daughters, one granddaughter, and two grandsons and lives with her husband in southern California. She is a court-appointed special advocate for the Voices for Children program, and her interests include reading and traveling.

A widely published poet and playwright, Bradley Steffens is the author of seventeen books, including *Free Speech, Censorship*, and *The Importance of Emily Dickinson*. He lives in Poway, California.